A N A H E I M
ANGELS

WORLD SERIES
CHAMPIONS

SP
SPORTS
PUBLISHING
L.L.C.

www.sportspublishingllc.com

SPORTS PUBLISHING L.L.C.

Publisher
PETER L. BANNON

Senior Managing Editors
SUSAN M. MOYER and **JOSEPH J. BANNON JR.**

Art Director
K. JEFFREY HIGGERSON

Developmental Editors
MARK ZULAUF, ERIN LINDEN-LEVY
and **NOAH AMSTADTER**

Book Design
JENNIFER L. POLSON

Cover Design
KENNETH J. O'BRIEN

Book Layout
JIM HENEHAN, GREG HICKMAN,
JENNIFER L. POLSON and **TRACY GAUDREAU**

Imaging
CHRISTINE MOHRBACHER and **KENNETH J. O'BRIEN**
Halo graphic designed by Kenneth J. O'Brien

Copy Editor
CYNTHIA L. MCNEW

CD-Rom Development and Production
CDRC GROUP

The reprinted articles and photographs were originally published through The Associated Press.
In some instances, the articles have been edited to accommodate space limitations.
However, whenever possible, we have included the articles in their entirety.

ISBN: 1-58261-591-8

CONTENTS

POSTSEASON

ANGELS HOPE SALMON AND ERSTAD RETURN TO FORM

BY KEN PETERS, AP SPORTS WRITER

Tim Salmon and Darin Erstad are healthy and hitting this spring, and that makes manager Mike Scioscia smile.

The Anaheim Angels mainstays, who hit in the heart of the lineup, both were hampered by injuries and slumped last season.

"I think they have a renewed feeling of being healthy and feeling good with where their swings are—and they're showing it," Scioscia said.

Salmon had arthroscopic surgery on his left shoulder and another operation to repair a ligament in his right foot after the 2000 season and didn't have time to build up his strength in the shoulder before spring training last year.

The Anaheim right fielder got off to a slow start in 2001 and never really started hitting.

A career .290 hitter who had averaged 30 homers

and 100 RBIs over his career, Salmon slumped to .227 with 17 homers and 49 RBIs.

Salmon, 33, is hitting above .350 this spring, with four homers and 17 RBIs.

"Last year, I couldn't hit a slider," said Salmon, who had trouble handling some pitches because of weakness in his left shoulder. "Now I'm strong enough to let the ball come to me and hit it up the middle."

Erstad hit .355 with 25 homers and 100 RBIs in 2000. Slowed by a strained ligament in his right knee and other nagging injuries, last season he hit .258, with nine homers and 63 RBIs.

Although it was obvious he was not perfectly healthy, he still played in 157 games. The Angels came close to dealing him to the Chicago White Sox over the winter, but the deal fell through.

Erstad, 27, has insisted this spring that he feels no resentment about the near-trade, saying, "It was out of hitting, not swinging the way you need to, it finally gets to you mentally."

Scioscia believes the players' dedication might have made their problems worse.

"Those guys definitely work as hard as any players I've ever seen. They have such a passion for the game and such a sense of duty to come out and play hard every day and that started to work against them because it was tough for them to back off," he said.

"To do the right thing would have been to back off and take a little breather and try to get healthy. By the time they were around to feeling that was something that would help, they needed more than a couple of days."

ANGELS PITCHING SPOILS RANGERS' HOME OPENER

GLAUS HITS FIRST HOMER OF SEASON

BY STEPHEN HAWKINS, AP SPORTS WRITER

In their first starts of 2002, Scott Schoeneweis and Ismael Valdes looked nothing like the pitchers who struggled so much at the end of last season.

Schoeneweis allowed just five hits and a run over 8 1/3 innings as the Anaheim Angels won 3-1 to spoil Texas' home opener and the Rangers debut of Valdes, the former Angel, who allowed five hits and two runs in eight innings.

"That was a great performance," Anaheim manager Mike Scioscia said. "Schoeneweis had to make good pitches all day. There was not a lot of leeway and he continued to do that."

Schoeneweis threw 66 of his 99 pitches for strikes and was effective with the change-up he has developed since last season, when he was 0-3 with a 6.75 ERA in his last eight starts during a stretch when the Angels lost 25 of their last 31 games.

Scioscia was equally impressed with Valdes, 1-7 with a 7.29 ERA in his last eight Anaheim starts.

"His fastball and his command were as good as we've seen it," Scioscia said.

As Rangers manager Jerry Narron said, "Schoeneweis was just better today."

Alex Rodriguez, Juan Gonzalez, Rafael Palmeiro and Ivan Rodriguez–batting in a row–were a combined 2 for 14 against Schoeneweis.

Troy Glaus, who has back-to-back 40-homer seasons, hit his first of this season in the seventh off Valdes. The two-run drive put Anaheim ahead 2-1.

Bengie Molina added an RBI single off reliever Colby Lewis in the ninth.

Even with 13 new players on their 25-man roster, the Rangers are in a familiar place: last in the AL West. Texas is 1-4, its worst start since 1991, and is back in the cellar where the Rangers ended the last two seasons.

"It's frustrating, obviously," said Rangers shortstop Alex Rodriguez, 1 for 18 with no RBIs. "We got a great performance from Ismael and we couldn't capitalize. I can't put a finger on it. We just have to keep grinding."

Schoeneweis, who struck out six and walked one, knew he caught the Rangers off guard with his new pitch.

"There's a little bit of uncertainty as far as a little bit of surprise," Schoeneweis said. "They are looking for a

FINAL

ANAHEIM ANGELS 3, AT TEXAS RANGERS 1

ANAHEIM	AB	R	H	RBI	TEXAS	AB	R	H	RBI
D. Eckstein SS	4	0	0	0	R. Greer LF	4	0	0	0
D. Erstad CF	4	0	0	0	G Kapler CF	4	0	2	0
T. Salmon RF	3	2	1	0	A. Rodriguez SS	4	0	0	0
G. Anderson LF	4	0	1	0	J. Gonzalez RF	4	1	1	0
T. Glaus 3B	3	1	1	2	R. Palmeiro 1B	3	0	1	0
B. Fullmer DH	4	0	1	0	I. Rodriguez C	3	0	0	0
B. Molina C	4	0	2	1	C. Everett DH	2	0	1	1
B. Gil 1B	0	0	0	0	H. Blalock 3B	3	0	0	0
J. Nieves 1B	3	0	0	0	M. Young 2B	3	0	0	0
A. Kennedy 2B	3	0	0	0	Totals	30	1	5	1
Totals	32	3	6	3					

HR-T. Glaus

Anaheim	000	000	201	—3
Texas	010	000	000	—14

Anaheim —	IP	H	R	ER	BB	SO	HR	ERA
S. Schoeneweis W	8 1/3	5	1	1	1	6	0	1.08
A. Levine S	2/3	0	0	0	0	0	0	3.37

Texas	IP	H	R	ER	BB	SO	HR	ERA
I. Valdes L	8	5	2	2	0	2	1	2.25
C. Lewis	1	1	1	1	2	1	0	3.85

"SCHOENEWEIS WAS JUST BETTER TODAY."

—JERRY NARRON

certain pitch in a certain area at a certain speed, and that's not exactly how I went about getting them out."

Al Levine got the final two outs, including A-Rod on a called third strike, for his first save.

Valdes allowed only a pair of singles in the first six innings before getting into trouble when Tim Salmon doubled leading off the seventh.

In his first game with the Rangers back in Arlington, two-time AL MVP Gonzalez singled leading off the second, advanced on Palmeiro's double and scored on a sacrifice fly by new Ranger Carl Everett, sliding under Molina's tag.

Gonzalez also made a lunging catch in right field on Garret Anderson's sinking liner in the seventh with Salmon on second. But four pitches later, Glaus homered.

"[SCHOENEWEIS'] FASTBALL AND HIS COMMAND WERE AS GOOD AS WE'VE SEEN IT."

—MIKE SCIOSCIA

ANGELS VICTORY BODES WELL FOR FUTURE

SPIEZIO STARTS SCORING OFF WITH THREE-RUN DOUBLE

BY JIM COUR, AP SPORTS WRITER

Seattle Mariners manager Lou Piniella is going to take a long look at demoting Paul Abbott to the bullpen.

Scott Spiezio had a three-run double in the opening inning and Tim Salmon hit his first homer of the season as the Anaheim Angels beat the Mariners 10-6.

"Sometimes a little stint in the bullpen doesn't hurt," Piniella said after Abbott lasted only 2 2/3 innings and saw his ERA balloon to 10.97 this season. "We'll think about it tomorrow and see what we do."

Abbott, who began the season as Seattle's No. 3 starter, was 17-4 for the Mariners last season. He gave up six

runs, seven hits and four walks in his fifth start of the season.

"We'll see what we do, but I want to emphasize that we have confidence that we'll get him turned around," Piniella said.

"Consistency is the key to the game and I am being consistently bad," Abbott said. "It's still early, but I'm concerned. The numbers speak for themselves. We've got a lot of guys out there with quality arms."

Abbott has pitched mainly as a starter the past two seasons after being in the Mariners' bullpen in 1999. He'd rather stay in the rotation.

"I want to take the ball every chance I get," he said. "But if that's what happens, that's what happens."

Anaheim won for the first time in seven games against the AL West-leading Mariners this season. The Angels broke a four-game losing streak and ended Seattle's four-game winning streak.

The Angels are hoping their victory means good things for their future.

FINAL

ANAHEIM ANGELS 10, AT SEATTLE MARINERS 6

ANAHEIM	AB	R	H	RBI	SEATTLE	AB	R	H	RBI
D. Eckstein SS	5	0	1	0	!. Suzuki RF	5	1	1	0
A. Kennedy 2B	5	1	0	0	J. Cirillo 3B	5	1	1	0
O. Palmeiro LF	6	2	3	0	B. Boone 2B	4	2	2	2
G. Anderson CF	5	2	3	2	R. Sierra DH	5	0	0	0
T. Glaus 3B	5	2	3	1	M. Cameron CF	5	0	0	0
T. Salmon DH	3	2	1	1	J. Olerud 1B	3	1	2	1
S. Spiezio 1B	4	1	1	4	C. Guillen SS	4	1	1	2
B. Molina C	5	0	4	2	D. Wilson C	4	0	2	0
J. DaVanon RF	4	0	0	0	M. McLemore LF	3	0	0	0
Totals	42	10	16	10	Totals	38	6	9	5

HR-T. Salmon   HR-C. Guillen

Anaheim	501	001	120	—10		
Seattle	000	001	320	—6		

Anaheim	IP	H	R	ER	BB	SO	HR	ERA
J. Washburn W	6 2/3	6	3	3	1	1	0	5.14
A. Levine	1/3	3	3	2	1	0	1	5.23
D. Cook	1	0	0	0	0	0	0	1.17
T. Percival	1	0	0	0	1	1	0	13.5

Seattle	IP	H	R	ER	BB	SO	HR	ERA
P. Abbott L	2 2/3	7	6	6	4	2	0	10.97
J. Halama	4	6	2	2	0	4	1	4.05
B. Fitzgerald	2/3	2	2	2	0	1	0	6.23
S. Hasegawa	1 2/3	1	0	0	1	0	0	0

A. Levine pitched to 3 batters in the 8th

"On paper, it looks like we have a pretty good team," Spiezio said. "But we haven't been playing like it. Sometimes when we've been hitting, the pitching hasn't been there and vice versa. I think if we put it together like we did tonight that good things will happen."

Jarrod Washburn (2-2) allowed three runs and six hits before being replaced by Al Levine with two on and two out in the seventh and the Angels ahead 8-1.

Bengie Molina had four hits, while Orlando Palmeiro, Garret Anderson and Troy Glaus each had three hits for Anaheim, which had a season-high 16 hits against Paul Abbott (1-2) and three relievers. The Angels' 10 runs also were their season best.

"Sometimes you're going to see the ball good for a while and sometimes you're not going to see that good," Molina said. "So it's kind of funny how that works. I was seeing the ball good today."

Anaheim came into the game hitting .199 (38 for 191) with one homer and 15 runs against Seattle this season.

The Angels took a 5-0 lead in the first inning on an RBI single by Anderson, Glaus' run-scoring single and Spiezio's bases-loaded double to right. Spiezio was thrown out trying to stretch his hit into a triple.

Spiezio came into the game hitting .224 with a homer and four RBIs this season. He hit .271 with 13 homers and 54 RBIs as Mo Vaughn's injury replacement last season.

"I know it's a long season and I've felt good at the plate the whole year," Spiezio said. "I know that it's going to come around. I was just trying to figure out if I should go to third or not and I shouldn't have."

They made it 6-0 in the third on Molina's RBI double, and Anderson added a run-scoring double in the sixth. Salmon's homer made it 8-1 in the seventh.

Spiezio had a fourth RBI on a fielder's choice before Molina's run-scoring single in the eighth.

The Mariners spoiled Washburn's shutout bid in the sixth on John Olerud's RBI double.

In the seventh, Levine allowed a two-run triple to Bret Boone before second baseman Adam Kennedy's error allowed Boone to score Seattle's fourth run, which was unearned.

Carlos Guillen ended Seattle's scoring with a two-run homer in the eighth.

MIKE SCIOSCIA • MANAGER

BY BETH HARRIS, AP SPORTS WRITER

Back in April, when the Anaheim Angels were off to a franchise-worst 6-14 start, naysayers crowed about it being another forgettable season for a team that hasn't made the playoffs since 1986.

If manager Mike Scioscia was panicking, he didn't let it show, resisting the kind of hasty moves triggered by losing.

"He keeps a positive clubhouse around here. He's always encouraging," said Tim Salmon, playing for his fourth different manager in his 11 years in Anaheim.

"It's been a long grind. It's been emotionally draining and physically draining," Scioscia said.

"The patience was the easy part," he said.

One of Scioscia's most respected qualities is his willingness to deflect credit to other people, particularly his players.

"You can put anybody here [as manager], and they're going to play just as hard. It's a good bunch," he said.

"I can't sit here and take credit for [Darin] Erstad diving for balls and going to walls or [David] Eckstein battling every pitch of every at-bat or Adam Kennedy breaking up a double play. That's their makeup and it's fun to be around."

At 6 foot 2 and 245 pounds, Scioscia still looks every inch the tough catcher who blocked the plate like few others during his playing days with the Los Angeles Dodgers.

He managed the Dodgers' Triple-A team in Albuquerque in 1999, then quit when it appeared he didn't have a future with Los Angeles.

A few months later, Scioscia was hired by the Angels despite his lack of big league managing experience.

But he did spend 18 years as a player and Scioscia remembers the pressure he faced every day. So as a manager, he's created an environment where his players can go out and achieve without worrying about getting punished for making mistakes.

"He gets on us when it's needed and he lets us go out there and play and go through our struggles at other times," Kennedy said. "If you've been playing well for the last week or so and you're not an everyday guy, he'll try to get you in there."

"He keeps guys sharp on the bench. We don't rely on one or two guys to win every day," Tim Salmon said. "He definitely includes everybody and he makes them feel like they're important and they're a part of what it's going to take to win."

Asked to define his managing style, the 43-year-old Scioscia demurs, believing it's about tactics, not style.

"The issue is what can your team do and what's going to be their best tools to win a ballgame," he said. "You want to put guys into positions where they can achieve and bring whatever talent they have into a game."

Angels 4, **Blue Jays 0** at Edison Field

PERCIVAL GETS SAVE TO PRESERVE SHUTOUT

APPIER NOTCHES SECOND WIN OF SEASON

Associated Press

Troy Percival has made a living out of making teammates hold their breath and opponents scratch their heads.

The Anaheim Angels' career saves leader escaped a bases-loaded, no-outs jam in the ninth against the heart of the Toronto Blue Jays' lineup to preserve a 4-0 victory for Kevin Appier.

It was quite a reversal of fortune for Percival, a four-time All-Star who surrendered a walk-off three-run homer by Oakland's Greg Myers last Sunday.

"He's one of the premier closers in the game," Toronto manager Buck Martinez said. "The impressive thing about Troy Percival is that he never gives in and he never gives up. He always believes he's going to save the game. He's a bulldog out there, and he's got the perfect makeup for a closer."

Percival relieved Al Levine with runners on first and second and walked Shannon Stewart. But the right-hander recovered to get Eric Hinske on a lineout to center field, then struck out sluggers Raul Mondesi and Carlos Delgado on 2-2 curveballs.

"We had the right guys up at the plate at the end of the game. But against Percival, it's a big challenge and a big hole to climb out of," Martinez said. "We're going through a tough time right now. We're not getting any big hits, but we'll keep plugging away."

Mondesi, in a 6-for-52 slump, said, "The guy throws 97-98, so I didn't expect he was going to throw

FINAL

TORONTO BLUE JAYS 0, AT ANAHEIM ANGELS 4

TORONTO	AB	R	H	RBI	ANAHEIM	AB	R	H	RBI
S. Stewart DH	4	0	0	0	D. Eckstein SS	3	1	1	0
E. Hinske 3B	4	0	2	0	A. Kennedy 2B	2	0	1	0
R Mondesi RF	5	0	0	0	O. Palmeiro LF	4	1	1	0
C. Delgado 1B	5	0	0	0	G. Anderson CF	4	1	3	1
J. Cruz LF	4	0	2	0	T. Glaus 3B	4	1	1	2
F. Lopez SS	4	0	1	0	T. Salmon RF	2	0	0	0
V. Wells CF	4	0	2	0	B. Fullmer DH	4	0	2	1
T. Wilson C	3	0	0	0	B. Molina C	4	0	0	0
D. Berg 2B	4	0	2	0	S. Spiezio 1B	4	0	1	0
Totals	37	0	9	0	Totals	31	4	10	4

Toronto	000	000	000	—0		
Anaheim	400	000	00x	—4		

Toronto	IP	H	R	ER	BB	SO	HR	ERA
M. Smith L	4	7	4	4	2	1	0	9
S. Eyre	4	3	0	0	1	3	0	9.14

Anaheim	IP	H	R	ER	BB	SO	HR	ERA
K. Appier W	6 2/3	7	0	0	1	5	0	3.49
D. Cook	0	1	0	0	0	0	0	1.17
A. Levine	1 1/3	1	0	0	1	1	0	4.63
T. Percival S	1	0	0	0	1	2	0	9.82

D. Cook pitched to 1 batter in the 7th

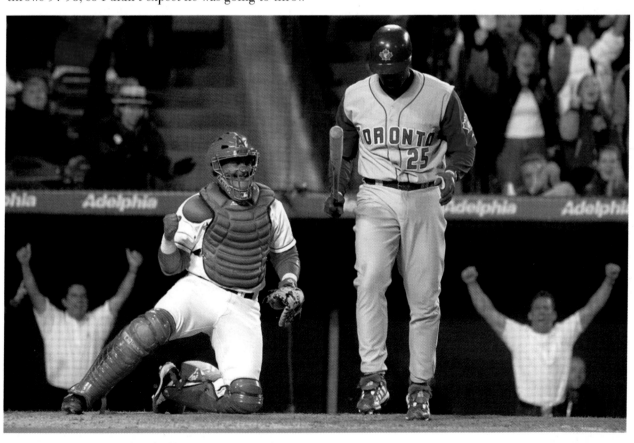

me a curveball at 76. He made a good pitch. There's nothing you can do about it."

Percival has no qualms about using his curve instead of his heater in certain situations, which helps account for his 213 saves over eight-plus seasons.

"I throw it in any situation. I don't care if it's 3-2, bases loaded, I'll throw it," Percival said. "I'd probably throw that pitch as much as I throw my fastball. I'm a two-pitch pitcher. If you don't throw them both, you're going to get in trouble every time, especially against those guys."

Appier (2-1) combined with three relievers on the shutout, the Angels' first at home since September 8, 2000.

The right-hander allowed seven hits over 6 2/3 innings, struck out five and retired the leadoff batter in every inning he pitched. Appier also stranded runners in scoring position in five consecutive innings.

"He's a competitive pitcher and he's not going to really give you much to hit," Toronto's Dave Berg said. "And if you do get your pitch and you don't take advantage of it, he's a tough guy to face. He's got all the pitches and he gets you to chase balls out of the zone."

Dennis Cook relieved Appier with two outs in the seventh and gave up Hinske's second double of the game. Mondesi reached on third baseman Troy Glaus' fielding error, but Levine retired Delgado on a fly to left to end the threat. In all, Toronto stranded 13 runners.

"We're not swinging the bat real good right now," Mondesi said. "We're trying too hard. We're trying to hit a home run every at-bat."

The Angels did all their scoring against Mike Smith in the first inning of his major league debut. Glaus hit a two-run opposite-field double in between RBI singles by Garret Anderson and DH Brad Fullmer.

Smith (0-1) allowed four runs and seven hits over four innings and hit two batters. He was 3-1 with a 1.54 ERA in four starts with Triple-A Syracuse and was promoted Thursday when the Blue Jays put right-hander Chris Carpenter back on the disabled list.

"THE IMPRESSIVE THING ABOUT TROY PERCIVAL IS THAT HE NEVER GIVES IN AND HE NEVER GIVES UP. HE ALWAYS BELIEVES HE'S GOING TO SAVE THE GAME. HE'S A BULLDOG OUT THERE, AND HE'S GOT THE PERFECT MAKEUP FOR A CLOSER."

—BUCK MARTINEZ

ECKSTEIN GRAND SLAM ENDS GAME IN 14TH

HIS SECOND GRAND SLAM IN AS MANY DAYS

Associated Press

David Eckstein came to the plate in the 14th inning muttering to himself about his six hitless at-bats.

He wiped away all those bad thoughts with his second grand slam in two days.

Eckstein's sixth career homer capped the Anaheim Angels' third comeback of the day as they completed a three-game sweep of the Toronto Blue Jays with an 8-5 victory.

"I was 1 for 7 today," said the Angels' 5-foot-8 leadoff hitter, who stranded runners in scoring position in the seventh and 12th innings. "I expect to do better than that, but I was very fortunate to get the game winner. It was about time I did something."

Troy Glaus started the rally with a single off Pedro Borbon (1- 2), and Tim Salmon followed with a double–his third hit in four at-bats after replacing DH Brad Fullmer as a pinch hitter in the seventh.

Scott Spiezio lined out to shortstop, and Adam Kennedy struck out after an intentional walk to Bengie Molina. But Eckstein drove a 1-1 pitch over the left field fence, extending Toronto's losing streak to five games.

"If you would have said a guy on their team would hit two grand slams in the series, I wouldn't have picked him," Toronto starting pitcher Brandon Lyon said. "But you see new things every day."

The homer gave Eckstein nine RBIs in two games after getting just seven in his previous 22. The game-winning grand slam was the first for the Angels since April 4, 1997, when Salmon hit one off Cleveland's Paul Shuey.

"He's the man," said Angels center fielder Darin Erstad, who returned to the lineup after a concussion that sidelined him for seven games.

"Eck's been coming up big in big situations. I think we need to have him hit the ball on the ground more and hit line drives–but we'll take those two grand slams."

Friday night against rookie Scott Cassidy, Eckstein hit the Angels' first grand slam at Edison Field in two seasons and had a career-high five RBIs in an 11-4 rout.

"Grand slams in back-to-back games is obviously rare–especially from a guy who makes his living playing 'little ball,'" said Angels manager Mike Scioscia, who was equally pleased about seeing cleanup hitter Garret Anderson go 4 for 6 with a triple and two doubles.

The victory went to the last of Anaheim's seven relievers, Mark Lukasiewicz (1-0). The former Blue Jays prospect, who never got out of the minors in his seven seasons with the organization, pitched the 14th inning and allowed an RBI single to Tom Wilson that gave Toronto a 5-4 lead.

Rookie Eric Hinske drove in his third run of the game with an eighth-inning double, giving Toronto a 4-3 lead. But he struck out against Lou Pote with the bases loaded in the ninth, squandering a chance to break the game open.

Blue Jays closer Kelvim Escobar, who got the last two outs in the eighth, blew his second save in five chances when Salmon homered to left center on a 1-0 pitch leading off the bottom of the ninth.

FINAL

TORONTO BLUE JAYS 5, AT ANAHEIM ANGELS 8

TORONTO	AB	R	H	RBI
S. Stewart DH	7	0	3	1
V. Wells CF	6	0	0	0
R. Mondesi RF	7	1	2	0
C. Delgado 1B	5	0	1	0
J. Cruz LF	4	3	1	0
E. Hinske 3B	6	0	2	3
F. Lopez SS	6	1	3	0
T. Wilson C	4	0	1	1
H. Bush 2B	3	0	1	0
a-D. Fletcher PH	0	0	0	0
b-D. Berg PH-2B	4	0	0	0
Totals	52	5	14	5

a-Hit for H. Bush in the 8th
b-Flied out to right for D. Fletcher in the 8th

ANAHEIM	AB	R	H	RBI
D. Eckstein SS	7	1	1	4
D. Erstad CF	6	0	0	0
O. Palmeiro RF	3	0	0	0
e-J. Nieves PH	0	0	0	0
f-J. DaVanon PH-RF	3	0	0	0
G. Anderson LF	6	2	4	0
T. Glaus 3B	5	1	1	0
B. Fullmer DH	2	0	0	0
c-T. Salmon PH-DH	4	3	3	1
S. Spiezio 1B	6	0	1	2
J. Fabregas C	2	0	0	0
d-B. Molina PH-C	3	1	1	1
A. Kennedy 2B	6	0	2	0
Totals	53	8	13	8

HR-T. Salmon, D. Erstad

c-Singled to shallow right for B. Fullmer in the 7th
e-Hit for O. Palmiero in the 8th
d-Singled to center for J. Fabregas in the 7th
f-Fouled out to first for J. Nieves in the 8th

Toronto	001	101	010	000	01	—5
Anaheim	010	000	201	000	04	—8

Toronto	IP	H	R	ER	BB	SO	HR	ERA
B. Lyon	6 1/3	4	2	2	1	3	0	5.9
F. Heredia	0	3	1	1	0	0	0	4.4
D. Plesac	1	0	0	0	0	0	0	4.7
K. Escobar	2 2/3	2	1	1	0	1	1	4.02
C. Thurman	2	1	0	0	0	3	0	3.45
P. Borbon L	1 2/3	3	4	4	1	2	1	4.76

Anaheim	IP	H	R	ER	BB	SO	HR	ERA
S. Schoeneweis	7	7	3	3	3	3	0	6.53
B. Weber	2/3	2	1	1	2	1	0	4.63
D. Cook	1/3	0	0	0	0	0	0	1.13
L. Pote	1	1	0	0	2	2	0	1.98
T. Percival	1	1	0	0	0	1	0	7.71
A. Levine	1 2/3	1	0	0	2	2	0	4.05
D. Wall	1 1/3	0	0	0	0	0	0	10.03
M. Lukasiewicz W	1	2	1	1	1	3	0	2.16

F. Heredia pitched to 3 batters in the 7th

"ECK'S BEEN COMING UP BIG IN BIG SITUATIONS. I THINK WE NEED TO HAVE HIM HIT THE BALL ON THE GROUND MORE AND HIT LINE DRIVES—BUT WE'LL TAKE THOSE TWO GRAND SLAMS."

—DARIN ERSTAD

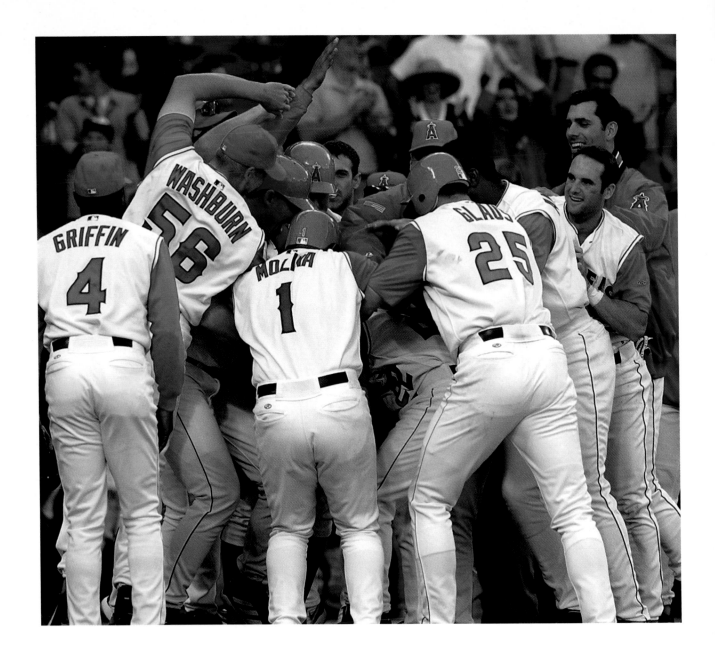

Anderson was on second with one out in the seventh when Felix Heredia relieved Lyon and allowed singles to his first three batters, including run-scoring hits by Spiezio and Molina that tied it at 3.

Hinske, who has hit safely in 10 straight games and 16 of his 19 starts at third base, made it 3-1 in the sixth with an RBI single. It was his first three-RBI game since opening day at Boston.

The Blue Jays are 8-15 with one game remaining this month. Last April they went 16-9.

"Nobody expected this. I mean, we didn't think we'd be leading our division right now, but I don't think we expected to have only eight wins," Shannon Stewart said. "We're in a tough little rut here and we seem to be losing in all kinds of ways."

ANGELS WIN EIGHTH STRAIGHT

ERSTAD'S THREE-RUN HOMER IN SEVENTH PUTS GAME OUT OF REACH

Associated Press

The slumping Toronto Blue Jays are helping the Anaheim Angels snap out of their early-season funk.

Darin Erstad hit a go-ahead three-run homer in the seventh inning as the Angels won their eighth straight Friday night with a 6-4 victory.

Garret Anderson also homered for the Angels, who reached .500 after starting the season 6-14. Anaheim hadn't won eight in a row since a nine-game streak May 31-June 9, 1998.

"Our goal isn't to play .500 baseball. We plan on being much better than that," said Erstad, whose team swept the Blue Jays in a three-game series last week.

Toronto has lost nine straight for the first time since losing 10 consecutive games in 1994.

"We are all struggling right now and it rubs off," pitcher Pedro Borbon said. "Bad pitching rubs off and so does bad hitting."

Borbon replaced starter Brandon Lyon (1-3) in the seventh and Erstad hit his only pitch over the right field fence, giving Anaheim a 6-4 lead.

Erstad had been 0 for 8 in his career against Borbon.

"That's not important. He's 1 for 9 now," Toronto manager Buck Martinez said.

Erstad said he was fortunate to make contact.

"He's pretty much abused me every time I've faced him," Erstad said.

Eric Hinske, Raul Mondesi and Homer Bush homered for the Blue Jays, who have lost six straight at home.

Angels starter Aaron Sele (2-2) allowed four runs–all on homers–and nine hits in six innings. He struck out four and walked two.

"I don't know if they are pressing. They have a veteran group of players over there," Sele said. "We all go through spurts."

Troy Percival pitched the ninth for his fourth save in five opportunities, getting out of a bases-loaded jam.

Percival loaded the bases with one out on Bush's single, an error by third baseman Troy Glaus and a walk.

FINAL

ANAHEIM ANGELS 6, AT TORONTO BLUE JAYS 4

ANAHEIM	AB	R	H	RBI	TORONTO	AB	R	H	RBI
D. Eckstein SS	4	0	0	0	H. Bush 2B	5	1	3	1
D. Erstad CF	5	2	2	3	E. Hinske 3B	5	1	1	1
T. Glaus 3B	3	0	0	0	J. Cruz LF	4	1	1	0
G. Anderson LF	5	1	2	1	C. Delgado 1B	2	0	0	0
T. Salmon RF	2	0	0	1	R. Mondesi RF	5	1	2	2
B. Fullmer DH	4	0	1	0	D. Fletcher C	4	0	1	0
S. Spiezio 1B	2	1	1	0	V. Wells CF	4	0	0	0
J. Fabregas C	4	1	1	1	F. Lopez SS	4	0	2	0
A. Kennedy 2B	4	1	2	0	D. Berg DH	4	0	0	0
Totals	33	6	9	6	Totals	37	4	10	4

HR-G. Anderson, D. Erstad   HR-E. Hinske, R. Mondesi, H. Bush

Anaheim	001	001	400	—6
Toronto	300	010	000	—4

Anaheim	IP	H	R	ER	BB	SO	HR	ERA
A. Sele W	6	9	4	4	2	4	3	5.71
M. Lukasiewicz	1/3	0	0	0	1	1	0	2
A. Levine	1 1/3	0	0	0	0	1	0	3.68
T. Percival S	1	1	0	0	1	2	0	6.35

Toronto	IP	H	R	ER	BB	SO	HR	ERA
B. Lyon L	6 1/3	8	5	5	2	1	1	6.11
P. Borbon	0	1	1	1	0	0	1	5.4
C. Thurman	1 1/3	0	0	0	2	1	0	2.95
F. Heredia	1 1/3	0	0	0	1	1	0	4.02

P. Borbon pitched to 1 batter in the 7th

But he struck out Carlos Delgado to end it.

"Carlos Delgado and Raul Mondesi are the heart of our order, but Troy is one of the best closers in the game," Martinez said.

Lyon allowed just two runs before the Angels scored four in the seventh. After Scott Spiezio led off with a double, Jorge Fabregas hit an RBI single to make it 4-3.

Adam Kennedy then singled before David Eckstein advanced the runners with a sacrifice bunt. Erstad followed with his homer off Borbon.

"I would probably throw him the same pitch again," said Borbon, who threw a fastball inside. "But when things are going bad, things like that happen all the time, and right now, we're all going bad."

Hinske hit a solo shot and Mondesi a two-run homer to give Toronto a 3-0 lead in the first.

Anderson hit his fourth homer of the season in the second.

Bush homered in the fifth, but Tim Salmon's sacrifice fly in the sixth cut Toronto's lead to 4-2.

"OUR GOAL ISN'T TO PLAY .500 BASEBALL. WE PLAN ON BEING MUCH BETTER THAN THAT."

—DARIN ERSTAD

FRANCISCO RODRIGUEZ • PITCHER

BY KEN PETERS, AP SPORTS WRITER

The kid with the electric arm did it again.

Francisco Rodriguez, the hard-throwing right-hander from Venezuela, again seemed completely unfazed by taking the mound in October against the storied Yankees. He's got two wins in the series and his major league career.

"I'm never afraid, never fear anything," Rodriguez said. "My father taught me that when you cross the line, it's supposed to be fun, and that's what I do.

"A month ago I was in the minors, not thinking I would be in the playoffs pitching against the Yankees. So this has really been fun."

Rodriguez, who came to the United States when the Angels signed him as a 16-year-old, explained that the man he considers his father is actually his late grandfather, who raised him. Also named Francisco, he died in 1999.

"Everything I do is for him and my mother," Rodriguez said, referring to his grandmother, Isabel. "I know she is watching all this on TV in Venezuela."

While the Angels' fans find Rodriguez exciting, so do his teammates.

"He's got an unbelievable arm," Tim Salmon said. "We've only known him for a couple of weeks now. The first night he threw, I went to [Darin] Erstad and we were just wide-eyed. He was just unbelievable with his stuff. That's what earned his spot."

With a fastball in the mid-90s and a wicked breaking ball, Rodriguez struck out Bernie Williams and Robin Ventura in the seventh, then got Nick Johnson and Juan Rivera as the red-clad fans in the sellout crowd of 45,072 stood and cheered every strike.

Rodriguez obviously has something special. In his 5 2/3 innings after being called up during the regular season, he struck out 13 and did not allow a run.

Anaheim manager Mike Scioscia said when he included the raw rookie on the first-round playoff roster that Frankie, as he calls him, was going to have an interesting week. That turned out to be an understatement.

"He's incredible. I think Francisco Rodriguez has that live arm that you don't see very often," Scioscia said after Friday's game. "He's got an incredible breaking ball, a fastball that just explodes.

"When it came down to it, we saw that Frankie had the makeup and wasn't going to be taken out of his game. Especially against a lineup like the New York Yankees, he's got the stuff you need to challenge those guys."

Angels 3, **Tigers 2** at Edison Field

GLAUS GOES DEEP FOR NINTH-INNING VICTORY

HIS FIRST HOME RUN AT ANAHEIM SINCE SEPTEMBER 29 OF LAST YEAR

Associated Press

It took 17 games for the restless fans at Edison Field to see Troy Glaus hit a home run.

Glaus finally went deep at home, leading off the ninth inning with his third career game-winning homer as the Anaheim Angels beat the Detroit Tigers 3-2 for their 10th victory in 12 games.

Glaus greeted Fernando Rodney (0-2) with a drive to left center field on a 3-2 pitch. Glaus' sixth homer of the season ended a drought of 82 at-bats at home without one since last Sept. 29.

"I was just trying to get a read on what his pitches looked like," said Glaus, who led the AL in homers two years ago. "After that, I was just trying to put a ball in play and make something happen to get the inning started. He threw a fastball and I was just trying to throw it out there. I didn't know it was out when I hit it."

One night after Seth Greisinger dueled Anaheim's Jarrod Washburn through seven scoreless innings, Detroit rookie Nate Cornejo was locked in a 2-2 tie with 14-year veteran Kevin Appier through seven before the bullpens took over.

Troy Percival (1-1) earned the victory, striking out the side in the top of the ninth. The Angels' closer has allowed only one earned run in 33 2/3 career innings against Detroit.

Percival couldn't believe it when he was informed that Glaus' homer was his first at home this season in 54 at-bats.

"I didn't know that–but he's always been there for me," Percival said. "Every time he gets up there, you expect something big out of him because you know what he's capable of. He's a clutch hitter and he never gets rattled.

"Every hitter goes into slumps, especially power hitters like that. They're going to have two or three weeks at a time where they're just not locked in. But I haven't seen any slowdown in him. I always have faith," Percival said.

Glaus led off the seventh with a double and scored the tying run on Bengie Molina's RBI single.

The Tigers took a 2-1 lead in the top half when Shane Halter and Wendell Magee both doubled between Glaus and the third-base bag.

FINAL

DETROIT TIGERS 2, AT ANAHEIM ANGELS 3

DETROIT	AB	R	H	RBI	ANAHEIM	AB	R	H	RBI
J. Macias 3B	4	0	0	0	D. Eckstein SS	4	0	1	0
R. Fick RF	4	0	1	1	D. Erstad CF	4	0	0	0
B. Higginson LF	3	0	0	0	O. Palmeiro RF	4	0	1	0
R. Simon 1B	4	0	1	0	G. Anderson LF	4	1	1	1
S. Halter SS	4	1	1	0	T. Glaus 3B	4	2	2	1
W. Magee CF	4	0	2	1	B. Fullmer 1B	3	0	1	0
J. Cruz DH	3	0	0	0	S. Spiezio 1B	0	0	0	0
D. Jackson 2B	3	1	1	0	T. Salmon DH	3	0	1	0
M. Rivera C	3	0	0	0	B. Molina C	3	0	1	1
Totals	32	2	6	2	A. Kennedy 2B	3	0	0	0
					Totals	32	3	8	3

HR–G. Anderson, T. Glaus

Detroit	000	001	100	—2
Anaheim	000	100	101	—3

Detroit	IP	H	R	ER	BB	SO	HR	ERA
N. Cornejo	7	7	2	2	0	3	1	5.1
J. Walker	1	0	0	0	0	3	0	4.15
F. Rodney L	0	1	1	1	0	0	1	6.75

Anaheim	IP	H	R	ER	BB	SO	HR	ERA
K. Appier	7	6	2	2	1	4	0	2.83
A. Levine	1	0	0	0	1	0	0	3.45
T. Percival W	1	0	0	0	0	3	0	5.4

F. Rodney pitched to 1 batter in the 9th

"I know that when I come up, Glaus comes in because he doesn't know if I'm going to bunt or not. So I think he might have been in a little bit more on me than he would have been," Magee said. "If I had seen him playing back and toward the line, I would have bunted on him to get Halter over to third that late in the game."

Garret Anderson hit his fifth homer in the Angels sixth.

Appier's scoreless streak ended at 17 2/3 innings, the longest by an Angels pitcher since Chuck Finley's 19 1/3 innings in April 1998.

Appier allowed two runs and six hits over seven innings, lowering his ERA to 2.83 in seven starts

since being obtained last December from the New York Mets in a trade for Mo Vaughn.

Cornejo allowed two runs and seven hits in seven innings and did not walk a batter.

"It was a good matchup between a veteran guy and a rookie," Detroit catcher Mike Rivera said. "Appier pitched a great game and Cornejo did the same thing. He just made a couple of mistakes when he fell behind Anderson and Molina. We went away from the plan that we had, but those are mistakes that we have to learn from so we don't do it next time."

ANGELS DESTROY WHITE SOX WITH "LITTLE BALL"

MOST LOPSIDED VICTORY AT HOME EVER

BY KEN PETERS, AP SPORTS WRITER

The Anaheim Angels' most lopsided victory at home started not with a bang, but with three consecutive bunts.

The "little ball" rally ignited an eight-run third inning, and the Angels went on to get 24 hits, five of them homers, in the 19-0 victory over the Chicago White Sox.

The win, the Angels' 12th in 14 games after a franchise-worst 6-14 start, was their most one-sided ever at home, and the 19 runs also were their most in Anaheim—or Los Angeles, where they played their first five seasons.

Adam Kennedy led off the third inning with a bunt single, David Eckstein bunted and was safe on a fielder's choice when the throw to second from third baseman Tony Graffanino hit an ump, then Darin Erstad bunted for a single to load the bases.

Chicago's Dan Wright then hit Troy Glaus to force in a run— and the rout was on.

By the end of the game, Adam Kennedy had homered twice and had four hits, Garret Anderson had homered and had four hits, and Tim Salmon also had four hits.

"The final tally, it's hard to believe it started with three bunts," Anaheim manager Mike Scioscia said. "All three of those guys have the capability of playing little ball."

Kennedy, who began the third-inning rally with the bunt and capped it with a two-run homer, said, "The bunt set everything up. It set me up for being more comfortable at the plate later and for us getting a nice cushion."

He said Wright probably was frustrated by the bunts.

"It's got to be frustrating for him to know that a ball hasn't gotten to the infield dirt and we've got three runners on, and then he hits a guy to bring in a run," Kennedy said.

Wright gave up eight runs and eight hits in 2 2/3 innings.

"I wouldn't say that he was rattled," Chicago manager Jerry Manuel said. "He just wasn't able to make the pitches to get out of it."

Overshadowed by the Angels' hitting barrage was the outing by pitcher Scott Schoeneweis. He held the White Sox to three hits in his seven innings.

"Everything kind of clicked tonight," said Schoeneweis (2-4), winning for the first time in his last six starts. "I threw everything kind of decent and their hard-hit balls were caught, and we scored 19 runs. I was getting kind of stiff between innings, but that's a

FINAL

CHICAGO WHITE SOX 0, AT ANAHEIM ANGELS 19

CHICAGO WS	AB	R	H	RBI	ANAHEIM	AB	R	H	RBI
K. Lofton CF	2	0	0	0	D. Eckstein SS	5	3	2	0
a-A. Rowand PH-CF	2	0	1	0	D. Erstad CF	4	2	1	0
R. Durham 2B	4	0	0	0	b-J. Ramirez PH-CF	3	2	2	3
F. Thomas DH	3	0	0	0	T. Glaus 3B	3	2	0	1
M. Ordonez RF	3	0	1	0	O. Palmeiro LF	1	0	1	1
J. Liefer RF	0	0	0	0	G. Anderson LF	4	3	3	4
P. Konerko 1B	3	0	1	0	c-J. Nieves PH-3B	2	0	1	0
C. Lee LF	2	0	0	0	B. Fullmer DH	6	2	3	4
T. Graffanino 3B	3	0	0	0	T. Salmon RF	6	0	4	2
S. Alomar C	3	0	0	0	S. Spiezio 1B	4	0	1	1
R. Clayton SS	3	0	0	0	B. Molina C	6	1	2	0
Totals	28	0	3	0	A. Kennedy 2B	5	4	4	3
					Totals	49	19	24	19

a-Singled to shallow right for K. Lofton in the 6th

HR-B. Fullmer, A. Kennedy 2, G. Anderson, J. Ramirez

b-Homered to left for D. Erstad in the 6th
c-Singled to right-center for G. Anderson in the 6th

Chi White Sox	000	000	000	—0		
Anaheim	008	233	30x	—19		

Chi White Sox	IP	H	R	ER	BB	SO	HR	ERA
D. Wright L	2 2/3	8	8	8	1	1	2	6.59
M. Ginter	2 1/3	7	5	2	1	3	1	5.68
M. Porzio	2	9	6	6	1	0	2	7.36
A. Osuna	1	0	0	0	1	1	0	5

Anaheim	IP	H	R	ER	BB	SO	HR	ERA
S. Schoeneweis W	7	3	0	0	2	1	0	5.08
M. Wise	2	0	0	0	0	1	0	3

good situation, to be sitting in the dugout while we're scoring a lot of runs."

Brad Fullmer, signed as a free agent in the off season, hit his first homer for Anaheim, a three-run shot, and Kennedy hit a two-run homer during an eight-run third inning against Wright (3-4).

Rookie Julio Ramirez hit his first major league homer, a two-run drive off Mike Porzio in the sixth.

Anderson, who hit a two-run double in the third, added a two-run homer in the fourth off Matt Ginter. Kennedy's second homer, off Porzio, led off the sixth.

The Angels sent 12 batters to the plate in the third. After Wright hit Glaus with a pitch, Anderson followed with a popup to shallow center that Kenny Lofton lost in the lights. The ball dropped in front of him and just over the outstretched glove of shortstop Royce Clayton, and Anderson was credited with a double and two RBIs.

Fullmer's homer was his first in 144 at-bats since September 18, when he was with Toronto.

Kennedy's homer in the third snapped an even longer dry spell—it was his first since last August 29, a span of 183 at-bats.

"THE FINAL TALLY, IT'S HARD TO BELIEVE IT STARTED WITH THREE BUNTS."

—ANAHEIM MANAGER MIKE SCIOSCIA

DARIN ERSTAD • CENTER FIELD
TIM SALMON • RIGHT FIELD

BY JOHN NADEL, AP SPORTS WRITER

Tim Salmon, Darin Erstad and the Anaheim Angels haven't waited forever to play in the postseason.

It only feels that way.

A starting outfielder for the Angels since 1993 when he won AL Rookie of the Year honors, Salmon has played in 1,388 games with 5,009 official at-bats.

"It's been a long time coming," said the 33-year-old Salmon, who bounced back from his worst season last year, when he hit .227 with 17 homers and 49 RBIs, to bat .286 with 22 homers and 88 RBIs this year.

"It's been really sweet, especially since we've been close a few times, had some tough collapses," he said. "It's been real nice to finally get there; it's been a great year."

The comebacks of Salmon and fellow outfielder Darin Erstad, who went from .258 with nine homers and 63 RBIs to .283 with 10 homers and 73 RBIs, has had a lot to do with the Angels' success.

Erstad and Salmon bat 2-3 in a lineup that led the majors in hitting with a .282 average.

"They've been huge," Angels manager Mike Scioscia said. "If you look at why we're in this position, I would have to say it's been our pitching staff. To support the pitching, we needed some key guys in our lineup to rebound. None were more key than what Darin Erstad and Tim Salmon did for our club."

The Angels lost 19 of their last 21 games to finish 75-87 last year and wound up 41 games behind the AL West champion Seattle Mariners.

Then, they started 6-14 this year and Salmon hit .182 in April.

It looked like another long season for both team and player, but it quickly turned around.

"I think the patience to see this lineup get together and play was what was needed," Scioscia said. "They certainly did after that 6-14 start; they've been incredible.

"I think it's a credit to these players keeping it together and believing in themselves. They had a terrific season."

A few years ago, Salmon considered leaving the Angels because he was uncertain as to their commitment to winning.

But he changed his mind shortly before the start of last season, signing a four-year, $40 million contract extension.

"When I re-signed, I saw the groundwork for a pretty good club," he said. "Going back to last winter, I said to myself, 'If I can get back on track and Erstad can get back on track, we've got the makeup to be there.'

"I really believed that going into this season. I think everybody believed it in spring training. You look at our lineup, one through nine, everybody contributes.

"I felt like we could be where we are today."

ANGELS BEAT TWINS IN 13TH ON SALMON HOMER

22ND VICTORY IN 26 GAMES

ASSOCIATED PRESS

Tim Salmon had a plan. Then he scrapped it at the last second and gave the Anaheim Angels another dramatic victory.

Salmon led off the 13th inning with a home run after Bengie Molina drove home the tying run in the ninth,

and the Angels beat the Minnesota Twins 4-3 for their 22nd victory in 26 games.

Salmon lined the first pitch from Jack Cressend (0-1) just inside the left field foul pole for his seventh home run. The Angels are 7-0 when he homers.

"I wanted to make this guy throw some pitches," Salmon said. "But then just as I got to the box, I realized, 'Hey, I don't really know what his other pitches are.' So I decided if he threw a first-pitch fastball, I'd swing at it. And he did. I don't typically like to swing at the first pitch, but it worked out in that situation."

Al Levine (1-1) allowed one hit over 2 1/3 innings for the win.

Denny Hocking hit a two-run double in the fifth and scored on a bloop single in the eighth by Cristian Guzman, giving the Twins a 3-2 lead.

But Molina pulled Anaheim even with a double that scored pinch runner Julio Ramirez after a one-out walk to Scott Spiezio. The hit came off Eddie Guardado, who blew his second save in 16 opportunities.

The Twins fell a full game out of first place in the AL Central. It's the first time in more than three weeks that Minnesota hasn't either led the division or had a share of first place.

"I don't worry about first place. First place doesn't mean anything right now. It means something in September. That's when we want to be in first place," Minnesota manager Ron Gardenhire said. "All I worry about is our ballclub playing good baseball and giving ourselves a chance to win games. We had the lead and we didn't finish the job tonight."

Orlando Palmeiro's second-inning double was the Angels' last hit off starter Matt Kinney until the seventh, when Kennedy and Jose Nieves singled with two out to chase the right-hander.

Salmon, pinch hitting for Palmeiro, hit a scorching liner that stuck in reliever J.C. Romero's glove as the pitcher tried to protect himself.

"The Fish is back," Angels starter Jarrod Washburn said of Salmon. "He hit that bullet in the pinch-hitting role and almost took that guy's head off, then came through with the big home run. We all have a lot of confidence in Fish, and he's back to being the Fish of old."

FINAL

MINNESOTA TWINS 3, AT ANAHEIM ANGELS 4

MINNESOTA	AB	R	H	RBI
J. Jones LF	6	0	2	0
C. Guzman SS	6	0	1	1
D. Mientkiewicz 1B	4	0	0	0
D. Ortiz DH	6	0	1	0
T. Hunter CF	4	1	0	0
C. Koskie 3B	5	0	0	0
D. Mohr RF	4	1	1	0
T. Prince C	4	0	0	0
a-A. Pierzynski PH-C	1	0	0	0
D. Hocking 2B	5	1	2	2
Totals	45	3	7	3

a-Grounded to second for T. Prince in the 12th

ANAHEIM	AB	R	H	RBI
O. Palmeiro RF	3	0	1	0
b-T. Salmon PH-RF	3	1	1	1
D. Erstad CF-1B	4	0	2	0
T. Glaus 3B	5	0	0	0
G. Anderson LF	5	0	0	0
B. Fullmer DH	5	1	1	0
S. Spiezio 1B	3	1	0	0
J. Ramirez PR-CF	1	1	0	0
B. Molina C	4	0	1	1
A. Amezaga PR	0	0	0	0
J. Fabregas C	1	0	0	0
A. Kennedy 2B	5	0	2	1
J. Nieves SS	5	0	2	1
Totals	44	4	10	4

HR-T. Salmon

b-Lined out to pitcher for O. Palmeiro in the 9th

Minnesota	000	020	010	000	0	—3
Anaheim	020	000	001	000	1	—4

Minnesota	IP	H	R	ER	BB	SO	HR	ERA
M. Kinney	6 2/3	7	2	1	1	5	0	3.65
J. Romero	1 1/3	0	0	0	0	0	0	0.33
E. Guardado	1	1	1	1	1	0	0	3.18
M. Jackson	1	1	0	0	0	1	0	0.9
L. Hawkins	2	0	0	0	0	4	0	1.95
J. Cressend L	0	1	1	1	0	0	1	6.37

Anaheim	IP	H	R	ER	BB	SO	HR	ERA
J. Washburn	8	4	3	3	3	7	0	3.47
B. Weber	1	1	0	0	0	0	0	3.79
T. Percival	1	1	0	0	0	1	0	3.29
D. Cook	2/3	0	0	0	0	0	0	1.29
A. Levine W	2 1/3	1	0	0	1	0	0	2.96

J. Cressend pitched to 1 batter in the 13th

"[WASHBURN] ALWAYS HAS GOOD STUFF. HE'S GOT A HARD FASTBALL THAT HE CAN MOVE IN AND OUT, BUT WHAT I LIKE ABOUT JARROD IS HIS TENACITY OUT THERE. HE GOES AFTER HITTERS AND HE DOESN'T MESS AROUND."

—DENNY HOCKING

Washburn issued fifth-inning walks to Torii Hunter and Dustan Mohr, both of whom advanced on a two-out wild pitch and scored when Hocking doubled into the right field corner for the Twins' first hit, tying it at 2.

"He always has good stuff," Hocking said. "He's got a hard fastball that he can move in and out, but what I like about Jarrod is his tenacity out there. He goes after hitters and he doesn't mess around. He gets 0-2 on guys and says, 'Here it is—hit it.' It works for him and keeps the defense involved, and that's why they make good plays for him."

The Angels opened the scoring with two runs in the second, but also got two runners thrown out at the plate. Kennedy doubled home the first run, and Spiezio scored on a bunt single by Nieves.

Kennedy tried to score behind Spiezio when third baseman Corey Koskie threw late to first, but Doug Mientkiewicz's relay to Tom Prince was in plenty of time. Palmeiro followed with a double to left, but Prince tagged out Nieves after the relay from left fielder Jacque Jones to shortstop Guzman.

Kinney allowed two runs—one earned—and seven hits in 6 2/3 innings.

Washburn gave up three runs and four hits in eight innings, tying a season high with seven strikeouts.

SCHOENEWEIS PITCHES GEM, RANGERS SHUT OUT

ANDERSON AND SALMON BOTH DOUBLE, PROVIDING RUN SUPPORT

ASSOCIATED PRESS

Scott Schoeneweis couldn't have come much closer to his second career shutout.

Schoeneweis threw 125 pitches before Troy Percival tossed the last four in a combined four-hitter as the Anaheim Angels beat the Texas Rangers 3-0.

Garret Anderson and Tim Salmon had RBI doubles to support Schoeneweis (4-4), who came within one out of giving the Angels their first complete-game shutout since Brian Cooper's three-hit victory over Oakland on June 30, 2000.

"Nobody was pulling for Schoney more than I was," Angels manager Mike Scioscia said.

The crowd of 16,810 gave Schoeneweis a loud ovation when he went to the mound in the ninth to face Alex Rodriguez, Rafael Palmeiro and Juan Gonzalez, who have hit more than 1,100 home runs combined.

Usually, the ninth is reserved for Percival, the team's career saves leader. But he had pitched in each of the previous three games, and Scioscia wanted to see if he could get away with keeping Schoeneweis out there despite the fact that he'd already thrown 110 pitches.

"It was a nice feeling to be out there in the ninth in that situation. There was definitely some emotions there," Schoeneweis said. "One of the things I pride myself on is durability and having a strong arm. I've been working on a lot of things, and they're starting to pay off."

Schoeneweis' only other shutout came in his second major league start. The left-hander retired Rodriguez on a foul pop, then got Palmeiro on a flyout before walking Gonzalez on a 3-2 pitch. Percival came on and retired former batterymate Todd Greene on a fly to the warning track in center field.

FINAL

TEXAS RANGERS 0, AT ANAHEIM ANGELS 3

TEXAS	AB	R	H	RBI	ANAHEIM	AB	R	H	RBI
G. Kapler LF	4	0	0	0	D. Eckstein SS	4	0	0	0
H. Perry 3B	4	0	0	0	D. Erstad CF	4	0	0	0
A. Rodriguez SS	3	0	1	0	T. Glaus 3B	4	1	2	0
R. Palmeiro DH	4	0	0	0	G. Anderson LF	4	1	2	1
J. Gonzalez RF	3	0	2	0	B. Fullmer DH	3	0	0	0
T. Greene 1B	4	0	0	0	T. Salmon RF	3	1	2	1
B. Haselman C	3	0	1	0	S. Spiezio 1B	2	0	0	0
M. Young 2B	3	0	0	0	B. Molina C	3	0	1	1
C. Murray CF	2	0	0	0	A. Kennedy 2B	2	0	0	0
Totals	30	0	4	0	Totals	29	3	7	3

Texas	000	000	000	—0
Anaheim	100	000	20x	—3

Texas	IP	H	R	ER	BB	SO	HR	ERA
D. Burba L	6 2/3	7	3	3	1	0	0	5.21
A. Telford	2/3	0	0	0	1	0	0	1.42
J. Alvarez	1	0	0	0	0	0	0	0

Anaheim	IP	H	R	ER	BB	SO	HR	ERA
S. Schoeneweis W	8 2/3	4	0	0	3	4	0	4.77
T. Percival S	1/3	0	0	0	0	0	0	2.6

"Schoney had some pitches left after the first two guys," Scioscia said. "He had a little leash there to try to see if he could nail it down, get the shutout and save Percy. But when he didn't, it was a decision we had to make."

The Rangers, who weren't shut out until the 161st game last season, already have been blanked three times this year—all in the last 28 games.

"Schoeneweis was outstanding," Texas manager Jerry Narron said. "We weren't able to string anything together or get anything going against him. We had one chance in the seventh, and he got a double play to get out of it."

Gonzalez had two singles, Rodriguez doubled and Bill Haselman singled for the other hit off Schoeneweis, who lost four of his previous five career decisions against Texas.

"I've always felt he's had good stuff, whether he had a good game or a bad game against us," Palmeiro said. "Tonight he had total control of the game. He had good movement

"TONIGHT [SCHOENEWEIS] HAD TOTAL CONTROL OF THE GAME. HE HAD GOOD MOVEMENT ON HIS
PITCHES, AND HE KEPT THE BALL DOWN. HE'S A TOUGH PITCHER TO FACE."

—RAFAEL PALMEIRO

on his pitches, and he kept the ball down. He's a tough pitcher to face."

Dave Burba (3-3), who entered 6-1 against the Angels with a 1.82 ERA, allowed three runs and seven hits in 6 2/3 innings. The right-hander, who leads the Texas staff with 48 strikeouts, failed to record one for the first time this season.

Troy Glaus, who came in 2 for 18 lifetime against Burba, snapped an 0-for-15 drought with a two-out triple high off the 18-foot wall in right field, and Anderson doubled on the next pitch. It was the ninth time in Burba's 11 starts that he was scored on in the opening inning.

The Angels got a pair of insurance runs in the seventh on doubles by Anderson and Salmon and an RBI single by Bengie Molina that chased Burba.

Angels 4, **Reds** 3 at Edison Field

ANGELS WITHIN 1 GAME OF SEATTLE IN AL WEST

TONE SET EARLY WITH FIVE HITS IN THE THIRD INNING

ASSOCIATED PRESS

A bad night got worse for the Cincinnati Reds.

Ken Griffey Jr. left in the fourth with a hamstring injury an inning after the Anaheim Angels scored four runs—sparked by Garret Anderson's two-run double—to beat the Reds 4-3.

With the Reds trailing 4-0 in the fourth inning, Griffey pulled up lame after hustling to first base on a fielder's choice grounder in the fourth inning. Angels team

physician Dr. Craig Milhouse examined Griffey, who is day to day with a mild strain of his right hamstring.

"It's not bad," Reds manager Bob Boone said. "It's not his bad hamstring. The doctor felt around and didn't feel anything. I'm hoping it just scared him a little."

Griffey returned to the Reds only two weeks ago after missing 41 games earlier this season with a torn tendon in his right knee. This injury is to the same leg, but it's a different area.

"It's bad enough," said Griffey who was limping and had his leg wrapped and iced. "I don't think people know how hard this is. I've gone through this for two years. I just want to play."

Aaron Sele (6-3) allowed two runs and seven hits in 7 1/3 innings to win for the sixth time in seven decisions. He struck out five and walked none.

The Angels have won 18 of 23 to move within one game of Seattle in the AL West. Since April 24, the Angels are 29-9, the best record in baseball.

FINAL

CINCINNATI REDS 3, AT ANAHEIM ANGELS 4

CINCINNATI	AB	R	H	RBI
B. Larkin SS	5	1	2	0
S. Casey 1B	4	0	1	0
K. Griffey Jr CF	2	0	0	0
R. Taylor PR-CF	2	0	1	0
A. Dunn DH	4	0	2	1
J. Encarnacion RF	4	0	0	0
A. Boone 3B	4	1	1	0
T. Walker 2B	4	0	2	1
A. Kearns LF	4	1	1	0
C. Miller C	2	0	0	0
a-W. Guerrero PH	1	0	0	0
J. LaRue C	1	0	1	1
Totals	37	3	11	3

ANAHEIM	AB	R	H	RBI
D. Eckstein SS	2	0	1	0
D. Erstad CF	4	1	1	0
T. Glaus 3B	3	1	1	1
G. Anderson LF	4	0	1	2
B. Fullmer DH	3	0	0	0
b-T. Salmon PH-DH	1	0	0	0
O. Palmeiro RF	3	0	1	0
S. Spiezio 1B	3	1	1	0
J. Fabregas C	3	1	1	0
A. Kennedy 2B	3	0	1	1
Totals	29	4	8	4

b-Struck out swinging for B. Fullmer in the 8th

a-Struck out swinging for C. Miller in the 8th

Cincinnati	000	010	011	—3
Anaheim	004	000	00x	—4

Cincinnati	IP	H	R	ER	BB	SO	HR	ERA
C. Reitsma L	7	6	4	4	2	3	0	2.92
J. Silva	1/3	2	0	0	1	0	0	0
G. White	1/3	0	0	0	0	0	0	2.7
S. Sullivan	1/3	0	0	0	0	1	0	3.51

Anaheim	IP	H	R	ER	BB	SO	HR	ERA
A. Sele W	7 1/3	7	2	2	0	5	0	4.89
D. Cook	1/3	1	0	0	0	0	0	2.12
A. Levine	1/3	1	0	0	0	0	0	3.18
T. Percival S	1	2	1	1	0	1	0	2.95

The Angels set the tone early with five hits in the third inning, capped by Anderson's opposite-field drive off Chris Reitsma (3-3). The Angels also got an RBI groundout from Adam Kennedy and an RBI single by Troy Glaus.

Reitsma allowed four runs and six hits in seven innings. The only hit he allowed outside the third inning was a bunt single to Orlando Palmeiro in the fourth. Reitsma retired the last 11 batters he faced.

"The only thing that went right for me tonight was it didn't rain," said Reitsma, who lost his third straight decision. "I felt I pitched a good game. It's one of those things in baseball where you just have to shake your head and laugh."

Troy Percival allowed a two-out RBI single in the ninth to Jason LaRue before earning his 12th save.

"THE ONLY THING THAT WENT RIGHT FOR ME TONIGHT WAS IT DIDN'T RAIN."

—CHRIS REITSMA

Angels 8, **Dodgers 4** at Dodger Stadium

ANGELS TRIUMPH IN "VERY STRANGE GAME"

ORTIZ ALLOWS FOUR HITS, ALL SOLO HOME RUNS

BY KEN PETERS, AP SPORTS WRITER

Anaheim's Ramon Ortiz gave up only four hits—all homers—in going the distance. The Angels scored three of their runs against Los Angeles on wild pitches. Four players were involved in two separate collisions on the same popup.

"It was a very strange game," Anaheim's Tim Salmon said after the Angels' 8-4 victory over the Dodgers.

Strangest of all, perhaps was the fact that the only hits Ortiz allowed were solo home runs. He has given up a major league-high 22 homers this season, and 18 of them were solo shots.

Anaheim manager Mike Scioscia wasn't bothered by the homers, two hit by Shawn Green.

"He pitched a terrific game," Scioscia said of Ortiz. "There are a lot of guys in the Hall of Fame who gave up a ton of solo homers. He manages to make pitches in key situations."

In his third complete game of the year and seventh of his career, Ortiz was tagged for one homer apiece by Eric Karros and Alex Cora.

Ortiz (7-5) struck out eight, walked just one and wasn't particularly bothered by the homers against him.

"When you're winning by seven runs, or eight runs, then you want to throw strikes," said Ortiz, who was staked to a 6-1 lead by the fourth inning. "We won and I'm happy. The home runs, that's OK. They hit some very good pitches."

FINAL
ANAHEIM ANGELS 8, AT LOS ANGELES DODGERS 4

ANAHEIM	AB	R	H	RBI	LOS ANGELES	AB	R	H	RBI
D. Eckstein SS	4	1	0	0	D. Roberts CF	4	0	0	0
D. Erstad CF	5	2	3	0	P. Lo Duca C	4	0	0	0
T. Glaus 3B	3	2	1	0	S. Green RF	4	2	2	2
G. Anderson LF	4	2	1	2	B. Jordan LF	4	0	0	0
T. Salmon RF	5	1	2	2	E. Karros 1B	4	1	1	1
S. Spiezio 1B	2	0	0	0	M. Grudzielanek 2B	3	0	0	0
B. Molina C	5	0	3	1	A. Beltre 3B	2	0	0	0
B. Gil 2B	5	0	1	0	C. Izturis SS	3	0	0	0
R. Ortiz P	4	0	0	0	K. Ishii P	1	0	0	0
Totals	37	8	11	5	G. Mota P	0	0	0	0
					a-A. Cora PH	1	1	1	1
HR-G. Anderson					G. Carrara P	0	0	0	0
					b-H. Bocachica PH	1	0	0	0
					T. Mulholland P	0	0	0	0
					Totals	31	4	4	4

HR-E. Karros, A. Cora, S. Green 2

a-Homered to right-center for G. Mota in the 6th
b-Flied out to center for G. Carrara in the 8th

Anaheim	003	301	001	—8
Los Angeles	010	002	001	—4

Anaheim	IP	H	R	ER	BB	SO	HR	ERA
R. Ortiz W	9	4	4	4	1	8	4	3.4

Los Angeles	IP	H	R	ER	BB	SO	HR	ERA
K. Ishii L	3	7	6	5	4	3	0	3.61
G. Mota	3	2	1	1	1	1	1	3.15
G. Carrara	2	1	0	0	0	0	0	4.42
T. Mulholland	1	1	1	1	0	0	0	9.19

K. Ishii pitched to 3 batters in the 4th

"[ORTIZ] PITCHED A TERRIFIC GAME. THERE ARE A LOT OF GUYS IN THE HALL OF FAME WHO GAVE UP A TON OF SOLO HOMERS. HE MANAGES TO MAKE PITCHES IN KEY SITUATIONS."

—MIKE SCIOSCIA

The Angels scored six runs on seven hits and four walks in three-plus innings against Kazuhisa Ishii (10-2), plagued by control problems.

Three Dodgers and Salmon were in two separate collisions on one play—when Salmon popped up foul between home and first base in the sixth inning. Salmon, running to first, collided with Karros as the first baseman tried to get to the popup, and Los Angeles reliever Mota collided with catcher Paul Lo Duca, who still made the catch. All four players remained in the game.

The Angels chased Dodgers rookie Ishii, who had won 10 of his 12 starts, off in his earliest exit so

far. Two of the Angels' runs against him scored on wild pitches, and he also threw off-target to second base to draw an error on a fielder's choice grounder in the third inning.

Nine of the first 16 Anaheim batters reached base against the former Yakult Swallows star, who had gone at least five innings in each of his other starts for Los Angeles.

"Let's give Kazuhisa a heck of a lot of credit—the guy's 10-2," Los Angeles manager Jim Tracy said. "He's done some wonderful things up to this point to get himself out of bad situations, and he darn near did it again tonight.

"If he had made the throw to second base, there are two outs and a runner at third and we're still ahead 1-0 in the third inning. Maybe the complexion of the game changes completely if we make that play. But it didn't happen."

Salmon had a two-run single to highlight a three-run third inning as the Angels took a 3-1 lead. The other run in the inning scored on a wild pitch by Ishii. Anaheim scored three more in the fourth, with one run coming in on Ishii's wild pitch, another on Garret Anderson's sacrifice fly, and the third on Bengie Molina's RBI single.

Anderson's solo homer off Guillermo Mota in the sixth stretched the lead to 7-1. Green and Cora homered in the sixth, and Green hit another, his 18th, in the ninth.

The Angels scored their final run on still another wild pitch, this time by reliever Terry Mulholland in the ninth.

Darin Erstad and Molina each had three hits for the Angels, who are 33-11 after a franchise-worst 6-14 start and are 39-25 for their best record ever after 64 games.

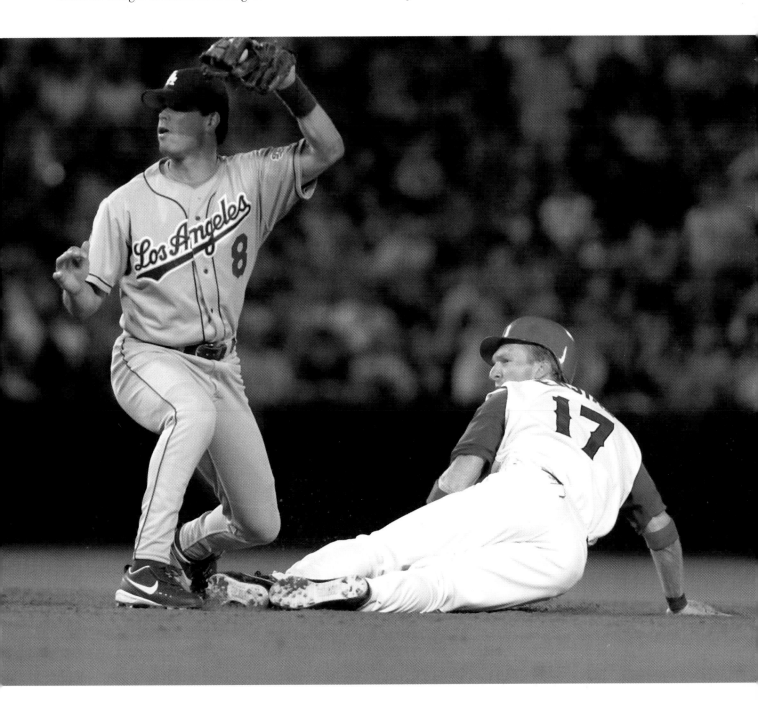

WASHBURN WINS 11TH IN A ROW, PITCHES TOUGH

ANDERSON HITS A TWO-RUN HOMER TO HELP LEAD ANGELS OVER TWINS

BY DAVE CAMPBELL, AP SPORTS WRITER

Even without his best stuff, Jarrod Washburn found a way to get another win.

Garret Anderson hit a two-run homer to help Washburn win his 11th straight decision and lead the Anaheim Angels over the Minnesota Twins 4-2.

Washburn, whose streak is the longest in the major leagues this year, set an Angels record for consecutive wins in a season. Chuck Finley has the overall club record—14 in a row from July 1, 1997, to May 2, 1998.

Throwing 128 pitches in six innings, Washburn (11-2) surrendered two runs, seven hits and two walks.

"Wash worked for it today more so than any other game during this streak," Anaheim manager Mike Scioscia said. "We talked about taking him out after the fifth inning, but he said he felt great and lobbied for one more inning. He pitched a terrific game."

Said Denny Hocking, one of five in Minnesota's lineup who don't usually start: "If we were going to get Washburn, today was the day to get him. It shows you what a tough pitcher he is. Even when he didn't have his best stuff, he was able to hold us down for six innings."

Troy Glaus drove in the go-ahead run in the sixth against Eric Milton as Anaheim ended a three-game losing streak.

Cristian Guzman had three hits and homered for the second straight game for the Twins. Batting against Ben Weber with two on and two out in the ninth, Guzman grounded into a fielder's choice to end the game and give Weber—with closer Troy Percival hurt—his second save.

Guzman's three-run homer in the eighth inning Monday capped a rally from a six-run deficit. Manager Ron Gardenhire was asked if he thought about his shortstop being the hitting hero for the second straight game.

FINAL
ANAHEIM ANGELS 4, AT MINNESOTA TWINS 2

ANAHEIM	AB	R	H	RBI
D. Eckstein SS	5	0	0	0
O. Palmeiro LF	4	1	1	0
T. Salmon RF	2	1	1	0
G. Anderson CF	4	1	1	2
T. Glaus 3B	4	0	2	1
S. Wooten DH	4	0	0	0
B. Gil 1B	2	0	0	0
a-S. Spiezio PH-1B	1	1	0	0
B. Molina C	4	0	1	1
A. Kennedy 2B	3	0	1	0
Totals	33	4	7	4

HR-G. Anderson

a-Grounded to first for B. Gil in the 7th

MINNESOTA	AB	R	H	RBI
L. Rivas 2B	4	0	0	0
c- D. Ortiz PH	0	0	0	0
C. Guzman SS	5	1	3	2
T. Hunter CF	3	0	2	0
M. LeCroy DH	3	0	0	0
b-J. Jones PH-DH	1	0	0	0
B. Kielty LF	3	0	0	0
M. Cuddyer 1B	3	0	0	0
D. Mientkiewicz 1B	1	0	0	0
D. Mohr RF	3	0	0	0
d-C. Koskie PH	0	0	0	0
T. Prince C	2	0	1	0
e-A. Pierzynski PH	1	0	0	0
D. Hocking 3B	4	1	1	0
Totals	33	2	7	2

HR-C. Guzman

b-Struck out swinging for M. LeCroy in the 8th; c-Walked for L. Rivas in the 9th; d-Walked for D. Mohr in the 9th; e-Lined out to second for T. Prince in the 9th

Anaheim	000	201	001	—4	
Minnesota	001	010	000	—2	

Anaheim	IP	H	R	ER	BB	SO	HR	ERA
J. Washburn W	6	7	2	2	3	4	1	3.03
S. Shields	2	0	0	0	0	1	0	2.81
B. Weber S	1	0	0	0	2	0	0	2.89

Minnesota	IP	H	R	ER	BB	SO	HR	ERA
E. Milton L	6	4	3	3	1	3	1	5.11
M. Jackson	1	1	0	0	0	1	0	2.54
J. Romero	2	2	1	1	1	1	0	2.13

"That's begging," Gardenhire said. "I try not to beg too much. He almost got one through today. He's swinging well. You like your chances when he comes up to the plate."

Less than 24 hours after the Twins' rally in a wild game filled with walks, errors and wild pitches, the Angels were victorious in a crisp game matching two of the league's best young lefties.

Washburn, who grew up nearby in western Wisconsin, had to lobby to come out for the sixth.

"I didn't know how many pitches I had thrown," Washburn said, "but I felt really good. I had too many foul balls in there. I'm trying to get through the hitters as quickly as I can."

Milton (11-7), turning in his fourth straight solid start after an inconsistent first half, lowered his ERA to 5.11 but missed a chance to move into a tie for the AL lead in wins. He gave up three runs and four hits in six innings.

Milton didn't bat against Washburn, but he lamented with the rest of his teammates about missed opportunities.

"I don't think today was one of his best days, but he was able to shut us down," Milton said. "You could tell he didn't have his commanding stuff. That's when you got to take advantage of a good pitcher like that and we weren't able to do it."

Hocking doubled leading off the fifth and Guzman hit a ground-rule double to tie the game at 2. Torii Hunter walked, but Washburn escaped additional harm by getting Matthew LeCroy and Bobby Kielty to pop out.

Milton couldn't quite get out of his jam in the sixth. With runners at first and second and one out, Anderson hit into a fielder's choice, but Glaus grounded a single through the hole into left to score Orlando Palmeiro and make it 3-2.

The Twins had Palmeiro picked off after his single, but the throw by catcher Tom Prince got past Luis Rivas at second base for an error.

Bengie Molina hit an RBI single off J.C. Romero in the ninth, giving Weber a two-run cushion.

Tim Salmon tied an Angels career record with his 282nd career double before Anderson's homer in the fourth.

"You can't have it back," Milton said. "It was just one mistake."

"WASH WORKED FOR IT TODAY MORE SO THAN ANY OTHER GAME DURING THIS STREAK. WE TALKED ABOUT TAKING HIM OUT AFTER THE FIFTH INNING, BUT HE SAID HE FELT GREAT AND LOBBIED FOR ONE MORE INNING. HE PITCHED A TERRIFIC GAME."

—MIKE SCIOSCIA

WASHBURN GETS 12TH WIN IN SWEEP OF MARINERS

ANGELS SWEEP AL WEST-LEADING MARINERS FOR THE FIRST TIME SINCE 1998

BY BETH HARRIS, AP SPORTS WRITER

The Anaheim Angels just won't let Jarrod Washburn lose.

Washburn won his 12th consecutive decision and

Garret Anderson drove in the go-ahead run with his second double as Anaheim completed a three-game sweep of the Seattle Mariners with a 7-5 victory.

"They did a great job. I just tried to keep them in the game, and they just kept battling back, scrapping every inning to put one on the board," Washburn said. "The bullpen did a great job after I got out of there."

The Angels swept the AL West-leading Mariners for the first time since June 16-18, 1998, at Edison Field. Anaheim moved within a game of first-place Seattle, which is two games ahead of third-place Oakland.

After winning the series opener 15-3, the Angels had to rally to complete the sweep.

"We just ran into a hot team," Seattle second baseman Bret Boone said. "They beat us pretty good this weekend, but we're not too worried about it."

The first two games were sellouts, with 34,945 fans attending Sunday.

"We had a packed house for the most part; the fans were into it," Washburn said. "I've never been in the playoffs, but it kind of felt like a little bit of a playoff atmosphere. It feels good to sweep anybody, especially Seattle."

FINAL

SEATTLE MARINERS 5, AT ANAHEIM ANGELS 7

SEATTLE	AB	R	H	RBI	ANAHEIM	AB	R	H	RBI
I. Suzuki RF	4	0	1	0	D. Eckstein SS	3	1	0	1
J. Cirillo 3B	4	1	1	0	D. Erstad CF	5	1	1	1
B. Boone 2B	3	1	2	0	T. Salmon RF	2	0	0	1
E. Martinez DH	4	1	1	1	G. Anderson LF	4	1	2	1
J. Olerud 1B	4	2	2	2	T. Glaus 3B	4	0	0	0
R. Sierra LF	3	0	0	0	B. Fullmer DH	4	0	1	1
M. Cameron CF	4	0	1	1	S. Spiezio 1B	3	3	2	0
D. Wilson C	2	0	0	1	A. Kennedy 2B	4	1	2	1
a-C. Guillen PH	0	0	0	0	J. Molina C	4	0	3	1
D. Relaford SS	4	0	0	0	Totals	33	7	11	7
Totals	32	5	8	5					

HR-J. Olerud

a-Walked for D. Wilson in the 9th

Seattle	000	401	000	—5
Anaheim	001	111	21x	—7

Seattle	IP	H	R	ER	BB	SO	HR	ERA
J. Pineiro	6	8	4	4	0	4	0	3
J. Nelson L	2	3	3	3	0	2	0	6.2

Anaheim	IP	H	R	ER	BB	SO	HR	ERA
J. Washburn W	7	8	5	5	1	4	1	3.22
B. Donnelly	2/3	0	0	0	0	2	0	3.21
S. Schoeneweis	1/3	0	0	0	0	0	0	5.45
B. Weber S	1	0	0	0	2	1	0	2.78

Washburn's streak is a career best. The Mariners rattled Washburn by scoring four runs in the fourth. Edgar Martinez's RBI single tied the game at 1. John Olerud followed with an RBI double. Mike Cameron's RBI single brought in the third run before Dan Wilson's sacrifice fly scored Olerud and made it 4-1.

"I didn't do my job," Seattle starter Joel Pineiro said. "I had a four-run lead and let them back in the ballgame. I gave up too many extra-base hits and too many two-out hits."

The Angels chipped away with runs in the fourth and fifth. Brad Fullmer's two-out RBI single scored Anderson, who had his first double of the game. Erstad's run-scoring groundout left Anaheim trailing 4-3.

Olerud hit his 17th homer on Washburn's first pitch of the sixth to give Seattle a 5-3 lead.

Adam Kennedy drew the Angels within a run on his ground-rule double with two out in the sixth.

RALLY MONKEY • MASCOT

BY CHELSEA J. CARTER, ASSOCIATED PRESS WRITER

At the House of Mouse, folks are going ape over a monkey. Toy monkeys have replaced Mickey Mouse as the most popular plush celebrity in town.

The Rally Monkey has become the unofficial team mascot.

"You kind of liken him to a baseball role player. He only comes out when he's needed," Angels'entertainment manager Peter Bull said. "Ultimately, the Rally Monkey is the belief that we can come back."

Rally Monkey was born on June 6, 2000, on the stadium's giant video monitor, when the Angels were playing San Francisco.

Trailing in the sixth inning, the Angels' staff played some video from the 1994 movie "Ace Ventura, Pet Detective" that featured a monkey jumping up and down. Then they flashed the words "Rally Monkey" on the screen. The crowd roared, the team went on to win—and the monkey became the mascot.

Today, fans haul Rally Monkeys to the stadium and keep them under wraps unless they are needed. Then they pop up everywhere—out of pockets, purses and from under hats.

The monkey's success has even spawned knockoffs, including the Indianapolis Colts' "Touchdown Monkey."

The monkey went 27-11 this season in games when the Angels trailed. The monkey's lifetime record is 57-41.

"He doesn't go beyond his boundaries. He has a time and a place to come out, and he does when he's needed," Bull said.

The Angels' staff tried bringing a live monkey to Edison Field. But the Angels lost, prompting pitcher Jarrod Washburn to accuse management of "making a mockery of the game."

Minnesota center fielder Torii Hunter even admitted Rally Monkey is a "star."

"Every time we go to their place, in the eighth or ninth inning, they always have a movie with him in it," Hunter said. "I forget I'm playing, I crack up. I turn and watch the whole show."

Rally Monkey Etiquette:

• The Rally Monkey may quietly watch the Angels only while they are at bat. That way, he can put his full attention on the way the pitcher delivers and pass the scoop on to the Angels batters.

• Rally Monkeys are not to watch or go crazy when the Angels are pitching.

• Rally Monkeys are to be "saved" until at least the seventh inning, after which one should expect a lot of monkey business. Remember, baseball is a marathon.

• At least one Angel runner has to be on base before the Rally Monkey can go into hysterics.

• Never stick the Rally Monkey in a plastic bag or it will kill the rally. The little guy needs respect!

ANGELS TEAM EFFORT DOES IN A'S

"ALL THE INGREDIENTS ARE STARTING TO COME TOGETHER"

ASSOCIATED PRESS

For the first time in Mike Scioscia's three seasons as manager, the Anaheim Angels have the pieces in place—solid pitching, excellent defense, timely hitting.

Aaron Sele allowed a run and six hits over seven innings and was supported by at least five outstanding plays in a 5-1 victory over the Oakland Athletics. One big play in the field was by right fielder Orlando

Palmeiro, who also had a three-run double off Tim Hudson.

Sele (8-7) walked none and struck out four. The only run the right-hander allowed came in the seventh, when Miguel Tejada led off with his 22nd homer and 117th of his career—breaking Eddie Joost's record for most home runs by an Athletics shortstop.

"All the ingredients in a championship-caliber pitcher—which is what Aaron is—are starting to come together," Scioscia said.

The Angels' 54 errors are the second fewest in the majors behind Houston. They sparkled in the field, particularly during a 1-2-3 second inning in which they turned three potential hits into outs.

After Palmeiro leaped in front of the 18-foot wall to rob David Justice of extra bases, third baseman Troy Glaus made a nice backhanded stab of Eric Chavez's grounder down the line. Shortstop David Eckstein then went deep into the hole to backhand Jermaine Dye's hard grounder to short before throwing him out.

Only two Oakland batters reached base in the first five innings, both on singles. But Tejada's double-play grounder erased Scott Hatteberg in the first, and Jorge Fabregas threw out John Mabry at second to complete a strikeout-double play with Greg Myers at the plate.

The great glove work continued in the sixth, when

FINAL
OAKLAND A'S 1, AT ANAHEIM ANGELS 5

OAKLAND	AB	R	H	RBI	ANAHEIM	AB	R	H	RBI
M. Ellis 2B	4	0	1	0	D. Eckstein SS	4	1	2	1
S. Hatteberg 1B	4	0	1	0	D. Erstad CF	4	0	0	0
M. Tejada SS	4	1	1	1	T. Salmon DH	4	0	0	0
D. Justice DH	4	0	1	0	G. Anderson LF	4	1	1	0
E. Chavez 3B	3	0	0	0	T. Glaus 3B	3	1	0	0
J. Dye RF	3	0	0	0	B. Fullmer 1B	3	1	2	0
J. Mabry LF	3	0	1	0	S. Spiezio 1B	1	0	1	0
T. Long CF	3	0	1	0	O. Palmeiro RF	4	0	2	3
G. Myers C	3	0	0	0	J. Fabregas C	3	0	0	0
Totals	31	1	6	1	A. Kennedy 2B	3	1	1	0
					Totals	33	5	9	4

HR-M. Tejada

Oakland	000	000	100	—1
Anaheim	002	003	00x	—5

Oakland	IP	H	R	ER	BB	SO	HR	ERA
T. Hudson L	7	8	5	5	0	5	0	3.48
J. Tam	1	1	0	0	0	1	0	6.26

Anaheim	IP	H	R	ER	BB	SO	HR	ERA
A. Sele W	7	6	1	1	0	4	1	4.73
B. Donnelly	2	0	0	0	0	2	0	2.65

second baseman Adam Kennedy made a diving stop in the hole to smother Myers' grounder and get the force at second on Terrence Long.

One inning later, Garret Anderson made a running over-the- shoulder grab of Chavez's drive before bumping into the lower fence in the left field corner.

"The defense is the key to a lot of our success," Sele said. "It gets overlooked, but when you can turn double plays and keep the extra-base hits to singles, it's tremendous."

Hudson (7-9) lost to the Angels for the second time in eight days, allowing five runs and eight hits in seven innings with five strikeouts. The right-hander entered the game 9-2 lifetime against

Anaheim and 6-0 with a 2.08 ERA in six career starts at Edison Field.

Kennedy, who failed to make it to second base on an extremely high popup that was dropped by Tejada in the ninth inning of Tuesday's 2-1 loss to the A's, led off the second with a bunt up the third-base line. He beat Chavez's throw with a headfirst slide to set up the game's first run.

"I agree that you get there faster if you stay up," Kennedy said. "Sometimes, instincts kind of take over and you're trying to reach and reach and get as close as you can."

Eckstein followed with an opposite-field RBI triple and came home two pitches later on Hudson's seventh wild pitch, the most on the Oakland staff.

APPIER SQUEAKS OUT A VICTORY AT SEATTLE

ANGELS TWO PERCENTAGE POINTS AHEAD OF MARINERS IN THE AL WEST

BY JIM COUR, AP SPORTS WRITER

Kevin Appier didn't enjoy matching zeros with Seattle's Jamie Moyer.

"No, that is extremely stressful," Appier admitted after allowing four hits in eight innings in Anaheim's 1-0 victory that moved the Angels back into first place.

Shawn Wooten's sacrifice fly in the ninth inning accounted for the game's run.

"That was the kind of game that ages you a lot," said Appier (9- 8). "I didn't like it except for the fact that we won. That was awesome."

Anaheim took two of three from Seattle to move two percentage points ahead of the Mariners in the AL West. The Angels have won six of the last seven meetings between the teams.

In the series, the Angels' pitching outmatched the Mariners' hitters. Anaheim outscored the Mariners 10-3 and out-hit them 27-15. Anaheim won 8-0 Friday night behind rookie John Lackey.

Appier and Moyer each pitched eight scoreless innings, with Appier improving his career record to 15-7 against the Mariners.

Appier, 34, who came to the Angels on December 27 from the New York Mets in a trade for Mo Vaughn, said he thought it might be a long, scoreless day when he saw who he was matched up against.

"We have a great offense, but, man, I've just seen him throw so many good games," he said. "He threw great today, too. Talking to the hitters, he was painting all night long."

Moyer lost a 1-0 four-hitter against Tampa Bay on May 21. But unlike Appier, he said he enjoyed tight, tense games.

"I'd rather be on the other end of it," Moyer said. "But that's baseball."

Mariners manager Lou Piniella didn't explain why he took out Moyer after eight innings and only 87 pitches. In fact, he didn't say anything. He kept his office door closed and didn't talk to the media.

Moyer was asked if there was a discussion about him coming out for the ninth.

"There was no discussion," he said tersely.

In the ninth, Mariners closer Kazuhiro Sasaki (2-4) replaced Moyer and gave up an infield single to Tim Salmon and a single to Garret Anderson. A wild pitch advanced the runners, but Sasaki recovered to strike out Troy Glaus.

Wooten followed with a sacrifice fly to deep center field to score the game's only run. The Angels have won three 1-0 games this month, with Wooten driving in the only run in two of those games.

FINAL

ANAHEIM ANGELS 1, AT SEATTLE MARINERS 0

ANAHEIM	AB	R	H	RBI	SEATTLE	AB	R	H	RBI
D. Eckstein SS	4	0	2	0	I. Suzuki RF	3	0	0	0
D. Erstad CF	4	0	0	0	M. McLemore 3B	4	0	0	0
T. Salmon RF	4	1	1	0	J. Olerud 1B	4	0	0	0
G. Anderson LF	4	0	1	0	B. Boone 2B	4	0	1	0
T. Glaus 3B	3	0	0	0	E. Martinez DH	2	0	0	0
S. Wooten DH	3	0	0	1	D. Relaford PR-DH	1	0	0	0
S. Spiezio 1B	4	0	2	0	R. Sierra LF	3	0	1	0
B. Gil 2B	2	0	0	0	M. Cameron CF	3	0	0	0
J. Molina C	3	0	0	0	D. Wilson C	3	0	0	0
Totals	31	1	6	1	C. Guillen SS	3	0	2	0
					Totals	30	0	4	0

Anaheim	000 000 001	—1
Seattle	000 000 000	—0

Anaheim	IP	H	R	ER	BB	SO	HR	ERA
K. Appier W	8	4	0	0	2	5	0	4.2
T. Percival S	1	0	0	0	0	1	0	2.08

Seattle	IP	H	R	ER	BB	SO	HR	ERA
J. Moyer	8	4	0	0	1	6	0	2.86
K. Sasaki L	1	2	1	1	0	1	0	1.57

He homered in the sixth inning of a game won by the Angels 1-0 in Kansas City July 11.

"I was just trying to hit the ball over Mike Cameron's head," Wooten said. "In the minor leagues, they teach you to try to hit the ball over the center fielder's head or down third base. [Sasaki] got a split up and I got a good swing on it. I just tried driving it."

Appier walked one and struck out six. Troy Percival, who came off the disabled list Saturday, pitched the ninth for his 23rd save in 25 opportunities. He hadn't pitched since July 11 because of an infected abrasion in his left Achilles.

"That was so much fun to watch the pitching duel between Kevin and Jamie," he said. "Those guys were outstanding today. You've got two really good offenses out there and to put up that many doughnuts was a great ballgame to watch."

Anaheim trailed Seattle by 10 1/2 games on April 23.

The Mariners got only one runner as far as second base in the game when Ruben Sierra singled with two outs and stole a base in the second inning. But Appier ended the inning by striking out Mike Cameron.

Moyer gave up no runs, four hits and one walk to lower his ERA to 2.86, fifth best in the AL.

The Angels threatened twice off Moyer.

With runners on first and third in the eighth, Moyer retired Darin Erstad on groundouts.

The Angels got two infield hits off Moyer in the third, but Cameron made a leaping catch after misplaying Benji Gil's line drive and Moyer retired Erstad on a groundout to end the inning.

The Angels are 19-11 in one-run games this season compared to Seattle's 13-17 record in one-run contests. Anaheim manager Mike Scioscia said he had a good feeling about the outcome all day.

"I think we're prepared for tight games," he said. "I think we have the type of talent on our team, especially on the pitching end, that's going to give us a better chance to win tight games than maybe a couple years before."

PERCIVAL REDEEMS HIMSELF, GETS WIN

SALMON HITS TIE-BREAKING HOME RUN IN EIGHTH INNING

ASSOCIATED PRESS

Thanks to Tim Salmon, Troy Percival got a chance to redeem himself after giving up a game-tying, three-run homer to Bernie Williams.

Salmon hit a tie-breaking home run in the eighth inning, and Percival retired four straight batters as the Anaheim Angels beat the New York Yankees 5-4.

"[SELE] COULD THREAD A NEEDLE TONIGHT. HE WAS KEEPING THE BALL OFF THE FAT OF THE BAT, AND THAT WAS BIG FOR HIM. WE DIDN'T REALLY GET A GOOD CUT AT HIM ALL NIGHT."

—JOE TORRE

SPIEZIO LEADS ANGELS AGAINST ORIOLES

SETS NEW CAREER BEST FOR RBIS

ASSOCIATED PRESS

Scott Spiezio has emerged as a major contributor during the Anaheim Angels' playoff chase.

Spiezio set a new career best for RBIs Sunday night, driving in four with a three-run homer and an RBI single as the Angels beat the Baltimore Orioles 9-3.

"I've always been a guy who believes in driving in runs any way possible," Spiezio said. "I've made some adjustments this year and I'm trying to do things a

little bit differently. It's paying off, and I'm just going to try to continue to do the same thing."

Spiezio gave Anaheim a 3-1 lead in the second with his ninth homer, following a leadoff single by Garret Anderson and a walk to Troy Glaus. Spiezio's eighth-inning RBI increased his season total to 69, eclipsing his previous best of 65 with Oakland in 1997. He has 20 in his last 21 games and is fourth on the club in RBIs—three more than Darin Erstad.

"The pleasant surprise with Speez is the way he's swinging the bat right-handed," manager Mike Scioscia said. "That's why his numbers have been a pleasant surprise. But there was no doubt in our minds from the outset of the season that he could knock in runs and contribute what he has."

Adam Kennedy capped a five-run eighth inning with a three-run homer, helping Anaheim win its fourth straight and 15th in 21 games. The Angels are 2 1/2 games ahead of Seattle in the AL wild-card race and 3 1/2 out in the West behind Oakland, winners of 18 straight.

FINAL

BALTIMORE ORIOLES 3, AT ANAHEIM ANGELS 9

BALTIMORE	AB	R	H	RBI	ANAHEIM	AB	R	H	RBI
M. Mora CF-RF	4	1	1	0	D. Eckstein SS	5	0	1	0
J. Hairston Jr. 2B	4	1	2	1	D. Erstad CF	4	1	1	0
C. Richard DH	3	0	1	0	O. Palmeiro RF	3	0	1	1
T. Batista 3B	3	0	1	1	b-A. Ochoa PH-RF	1	0	0	0
J. Conine 1B	4	1	1	0	G. Anderson LF	3	2	1	0
J. Gibbons RF	4	0	2	1	T. Glaus 3B	2	2	1	0
C. Singleton PR-CF	0	0	0	0	S. Wooten 1B	0	0	0	0
M. Cordova LF	4	0	2	0	S. Spiezio 1B-3B	4	2	2	4
B. Fordyce C	3	0	1	0	B. Fullmer DH	3	1	1	1
a-L. Lopez PH	1	0	0	0	B. Molina C	3	0	0	0
M. Bordick SS	3	0	0	0	A. Kennedy 2B	4	1	1	3
Totals	33	3	11	3	Totals	32	9	9	9

HR-J. Hairston

HR-S.Spezio, A. Kennedy

a-Struck out swinging for B. Fordyce in the 9th

b-Grounded to third for O. Palmiero in the 9th

Baltimore	100	001	010	—3
Anaheim	030	010	05x	—9

Baltimore	IP	H	R	ER	BB	SO	HR	ERA
R. Lopez L	6 2/3	6	4	4	3	4	1	3.39
B. Ryan	2/3	0	1	1	1	0	0	4.91
W. Roberts	1/3	2	3	3	0	0	0	3.01
B. Groom	1/3	1	1	1	0	0	1	1.69

Anaheim	IP	H	R	ER	BB	SO	HR	ERA
J. Lackey W	5 1/3	6	2	2	1	4	1	3.24
B. Donnelly	2/3	0	0	0	1	1	0	2.5
B. Weber	1 2/3	4	1	1	0	1	0	2.84
S. Schoeneweis	0	1	0	0	0	0	0	5.04
T. Percival S	1 1/3	0	0	0	0	2	0	1.96

S. Schoeneweis pitched to 1 batter in the 8th

The Angels, who won three division titles but never a pennant in their previous 41 seasons of existence, improved to a club-record 28 games over .500 (82-54).

"The whole order has been doing a great job," Spiezio said after the Angels completed their first three-game sweep of the Orioles in nine years. "I think the big thing is getting key hits in key situations with guys in scoring positions."

John Lackey (7-3) won for the fifth time in six decisions. He gave up two runs and six hits in 5 1/3 innings and struck out four, helping send the Orioles to their ninth straight loss.

"We'll get through this and get out of it, and we'll be OK," Baltimore manager Mike Hargrove said. "Right now, it's ugly. Every little glitch and every little mistake that you make is magnified. But at least we didn't beat ourselves tonight, which is what we've done pretty regularly in these past nine games. It'll be good to get home, you bet."

Lackey departed with a 4-1 lead and the bases loaded before Brendan Donnelly came on and walked Chris Richard to force in a run. Donnelly had stranded all 21 previous runners he inherited this season and retired his first batter in 28 of 31 appearances.

"The two things every reliever takes pride in is getting the first batter he faces and keeping the other people's runners on base," Donnelly said. "A lot of it has had to do with quality defensive plays after I've come into the game."

Baltimore put runners at second and third in the seventh against Ben Weber, who escaped the jam by striking out Melvin Mora and retiring Jerry Hairston on a groundout.

Scott Schoeneweis surrendered a two-out double by Jeff Conine and a bloop RBI single by Jay Gibbons, trimming Anaheim's lead to a run in the eighth. But Troy Percival got four outs for his 32nd save in 36 attempts.

The Angels made it 4-1 in the fifth when Erstad singled, stole second and scored on Orlando Palmeiro's double. Spiezio and Brad Fullmer had RBI singles in the eighth against Willis Roberts and Kennedy greeted Buddy Groom with his fifth homer this season—all of them coming at Edison Field.

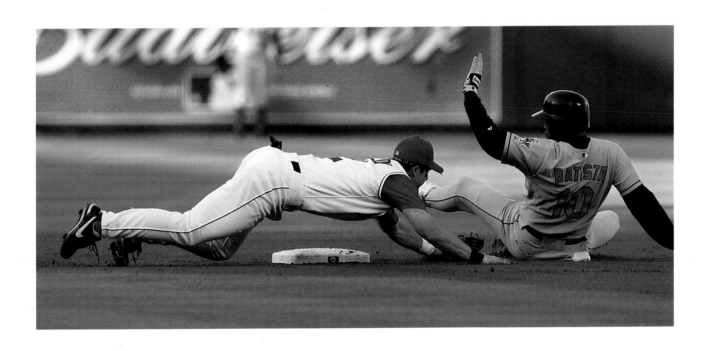

JARROD WASHBURN • PITCHER

BY BETH HARRIS, AP SPORTS WRITER

Angels pitcher Jarrod Washburn isn't feeling the pressure of owning a 12-game winning streak.

The stress is on his Anaheim teammates, who feel compelled to supply the offense so they don't spoil Washburn's run.

"We don't want to let Jarrod down," shortstop David Eckstein said. "He's the one going out and throwing the ball, but we take a little pride in what he's doing right now."

"I try to remember the last loss to keep me motivated because I don't like feeling that way," Washburn said. "Guys have been playing great behind me, so luckily we've been winning."

"This is a hot team. Everything they're doing is working out great," Mariners second baseman Bret Boone said. "They're swinging the bats great and they're pitching good, and they got the job done in every situation."

Much of the credit goes to Washburn.

"Jarrod is awesome," Eckstein said. "He goes out there and throws a lot of strikes and keeps the pace up, so that helps out everything. His intensity and competitiveness is tough to match."

"What's important to him is how you're seen by your peers, not only your teammates, but the guys you play against. I've heard an abundance of quality comments about Wash from other managers, pitching coaches, other major league coaches and players. They know what's going on with Wash," Black said.

One of the keys to Washburn's success is his health.

Last season, he was bothered by a slight break in a shoulder bone that doctors had a tough time diagnosing. In 2000, he was plagued by nagging injuries.

"He's continually working on his delivery, making it not so, I don't want to say violent, but he puts a lot of effort into throwing the ball," Black said.""He's toned it down quite a bit."

During the streak, Washburn's locker has become a popular place in the Angels clubhouse. The Wisconsin native happily obliges everyone who stops by.

"It's a little bit busier, but I don't complain," he said. "It's better than losing."

GLAUS HOMERS TWICE TO SUBDUE BALTIMORE

ANGELS WIN 10TH STRAIGHT

BY DAVID GINSBURG, AP SPORTS WRITER

Troy Glaus finally made a sizeable contribution to the Anaheim Angels' impressive winning streak.

Glaus hit a tie-breaking three-run homer in the sixth inning and added a solo shot in the eighth as Anaheim won its 10th straight, 6-2 over the skidding Baltimore Orioles.

The Angels' winning streak, one short of matching the franchise record, gives them plenty of momentum

heading into an important four-game home series against AL West-leading Oakland.

"They're a great team and we're a great team," said Darin Erstad, who had two of Anaheim's 12 hits. "What a great run they had. It will be a lot of fun."

Glaus' first homer gave Anaheim a 4-1 lead against Pat Hentgen (0-1), who was making his first appearance since May 2001, after undergoing elbow ligament replacement surgery.

"He's a good home run hitter. I made a mistake and he made me pay," Hentgen said. "Unfortunately, that was the game."

"Every day it's been a different person who lifts us up. Luckily, today was my day," Glaus said. "I haven't done a whole heck of a lot over the last five or six days, but we pick each other up. We don't count on one or two guys."

He added his 24th of the season against Rick Bauer. It was Glaus' second multihomer game of the year and the 14th of his career.

"Troy Glaus is one of the premier power hitters in the league today. Anybody who's got power

FINAL

ANAHEIM ANGELS 6, AT BALTIMORE ORIOLES 2

ANAHEIM	AB	R	H	RBI
D. Eckstein SS	5	1	3	0
D. Erstad CF	5	0	2	0
T. Salmon DH	4	0	0	0
G. Anderson LF	4	1	1	0
S. Spiezio 1B	4	1	1	0
T. Glaus 3B	4	2	2	4
A. Kennedy 2B	4	0	0	0
B. Molina C	4	1	2	1
O. Palmeiro RF	3	0	1	0
Totals	37	6	12	5

HR-T. Glaus 2, B. Molina

BALTIMORE	AB	R	H	RBI
J. Hairston Jr. 2B	3	1	1	0
M. Mora CF	3	0	0	1
J. Conine 1B	2	0	0	1
T. Batista DH	4	0	1	0
M. Cordova LF	4	0	0	0
J. Leon 3B	4	1	2	0
M. Bordick SS	4	0	1	0
B. Fordyce C	2	0	0	0
b-L. Lopez PH	1	0	0	0
L. Matos RF	2	0	0	0
a-L. Bigbie PH-RF	2	0	0	0
Totals	31	2	5	2

a-Flied out to center for L. Matos in the 7th
b-Grounded out to second for B. Fordyce in the 9th

Anaheim	001	004	010	—6
Baltimore	001	000	100	—2

Anaheim	IP	H	R	ER	BB	SO	HR	ERA
J. Washburn W	6	3	1	1	2	2	0	3.32
A. Levine	2/3	1	1	1	2	0	0	3.81
B. Weber S	2 1/3	1	0	0	1	0	0	2.69

Baltimore	IP	H	R	ER	BB	SO	HR	ERA
P. Hentgen L	5 1/3	9	5	4	1	1	2	6.75
R. Bauer	2 2/3	2	1	1	1	0	1	4.38
B. Ryan	1	1	0	0	0	1	0	4.86

"[GLAUS] IS A GOOD HOME RUN HITTER. I MADE A MISTAKE AND HE MADE ME PAY.
UNFORTUNATELY, THAT WAS THE GAME."

—PAT HENTGEN

like that is a land mine, whether he's 0 for 19 or 0 for 1," Orioles manager Mike Hargrove said.

Bengie Molina also homered for Anaheim, which completed its first three-game sweep in Baltimore since the Angels franchise was created in 1961. The victory also concluded the Angels' first 6-0 road trip since April 1979.

"We came out on this road trip with the idea that we needed to win all six to give ourselves the best opportunity down the last 20 games," Glaus said. "We've accomplished that."

Jarrod Washburn (17-5) allowed one run and three hits in six innings. The left-hander, who retired 11 straight at one point, picked up his club-record 13th road win and became the Angels' first 17-game winner since 1991.

Ben Weber walked in a run in the seventh before retiring Jeff Conine on a fly ball with the bases loaded and two outs. Weber finished for his seventh save.

Hentgen, the 1996 Cy Young winner, was activated from the 60-day disabled list before the game. He kept pace with Washburn until the sixth, when Garret Anderson reached on an error and Scott Spiezio singled ahead of Glaus' drive.

One out later, Molina ended Hentgen's return with his fourth homer of the year.

"It's disappointing, and a little frustrating," Hentgen said.

The Orioles have lost 14 of 15, with six of the defeats coming against Anaheim.

"We're in a stretch where every mistake we make hurts us," Hargrove said.

Both teams failed to capitalize on early scoring chances. Anderson hit a leadoff triple in the second, but was erased at the plate on Glaus' grounder to short.

The Orioles wasted two first-inning walks and Mike Bordick's one-out double in the second.

Anaheim broke through in the third. After David Eckstein beat out a two-out bunt to extend his career-high hitting streak to 15 games, Erstad singled and Hentgen let in a run with a wild pitch.

In the bottom half, Jerry Hairston hit a leadoff double and took third with one out before Conine tied it with a sacrifice fly, his club-high ninth of the season.

PITCHING DUEL ENDS IN ANGELS VICTORY

SALMON'S 10TH-INNING HOME RUN GIVES ANAHEIM EDGE

BY GREG BEACHAM, AP SPORTS WRITER

An exceptional pitching duel ended with one emphatic swing of Tim Salmon's bat, and the Anaheim Angels inched ahead once again in the race for the AL West title.

After Mark Mulder and Jarrod Washburn pitched to a scoreless draw through nine innings, Salmon homered in the 10th as the Angels reclaimed sole possession of first place with a 1-0 victory over the Oakland Athletics on Tuesday night.

Salmon's one-out shot against closer Billy Koch (10-4) decided a game that left both teams thrilled and drained by the battle between two of the AL's premier left-handers.

"I've never been to the playoffs, but I can't imagine anything much more adrenaline-filled than this," said Angels closer Troy Percival, who pitched the 10th for his 250th career save. "That was probably the best-pitched ballgame on both sides I've ever seen. Both guys didn't miss a spot all night."

Mulder, a 17-game winner, tied his career-high with 12 strikeouts for Oakland, allowing five hits over nine innings. He was matched for eight innings by 18-game winner Washburn, who yielded three hits while pitching on three days' rest.

Neither pitcher walked a batter, and Washburn didn't allow a runner past first base. Fans at the Coliseum

stood and applauded both pitchers in the late innings as the tension became almost palpable.

"It's never something you wish for, to be in a battle like that, but it was a lot of fun out there," said Washburn, who felt no ill effects from returning early. "I'm never dominant, but it was just about the best game I've pitched all year. It was definitely one of the highlights of my career so far."

Koch, who won for Oakland on Monday night, relieved Mulder to start the 10th. Salmon worked a full count before hitting his 20th homer of the season deep into the elevated left field stands.

"It wouldn't have gone out—if the fence was 100 feet back," Koch said with a grimace. "He absolutely crushed that ball. My luck ran out. Before I went in, I was thinking, 'This is a good game. I don't want to be the goat.' After he hit that ball, I thought, 'Damn, I am the goat.'"

Salmon, who was hitting just .162 in September, was actually grateful to face Koch's 95 mph fastballs.

FINAL

ANAHEIM ANGELS 1, AT OAKLAND A'S 0

ANAHEIM	AB	R	H	RBI
D. Eckstein SS	5	0	0	0
D. Erstad CF	4	0	1	0
S. Spiezio 1B	4	0	1	0
G. Anderson LF	4	0	0	0
T. Glaus 3B	4	0	0	0
S. Wooten DH	4	0	1	0
T. Salmon RF	4	1	1	1
A. Ochoa RF	0	0	0	0
B. Molina C	4	0	1	0
A. Kennedy 2B	4	0	2	0
Totals	37	1	7	1

HR-T. Salmon

OAKLAND	AB	R	H	RBI
R. Durham DH	4	0	0	0
M. Ellis 2B	4	0	2	0
M. Tejada SS	4	0	0	0
E. Chavez 3B	4	0	0	0
J. Dye RF	4	0	1	0
D. Justice LF	3	0	0	0
E. Byrnes PR	0	0	0	0
R. Velarde 1B	3	0	0	0
a-G. Myers PH	1	0	0	0
T. Long CF	4	0	0	0
R. Hernandez C	3	0	0	0
Totals	34	0	3	0

a-Flied out to deep center for R. Velarde in the 10th

Anaheim	000	000	000	1 —1
Oakland	000	000	000	0 —0

Anaheim	IP	H	R	ER	BB	SO	HR	ERA
J. Washburn	8	3	0	0	0	4	0	3.11
B. Weber W	1	0	0	0	0	0	0	2.49
T. Percival S	1	0	0	0	1	1	0	1.66

Oakland	IP	H	R	ER	BB	SO	HR	ERA
M. Mulder	9	5	0	0	0	12	0	3.57
B. Koch L	1	2	1	1	0	2	1	2.94

"IT WOULDN'T HAVE GONE OUT—IF THE FENCE WAS 100 FEET BACK.
[SALMON] ABSOLUTELY CRUSHED THAT BALL."
—BILLY KOCH

"Mulder had me baffled," Salmon said. "The guy had everything working. ... It feels great to get the big one in a game like this. I've played my whole career for this. I can't imagine more intensity than there was out there tonight."

Ben Weber (7-2) pitched the ninth for the win. Percival allowed a base runner in the 10th, but he finished strong for his 40th save in 44 chances as Anaheim won for the 17th time in 19 games.

"That was a great baseball game, almost a throwback game, like Marichal and Koufax going at it," Oakland manager Art Howe said.

After Oakland (94-57) climbed back into a first-place tie with a win over the Angels on Monday night, Anaheim (95-56) returned the favor in a four-game series that has big implications on baseball's tightest division race.

Five of their six meetings over the past nine days were decided by one run.

The Angels haven't won a division title or been to the postseason since 1986, while the A's are looking for their second AL West crown in three

seasons. Both teams will almost certainly be in the playoffs, but both would prefer the home-field advantage that comes with the division title.

Washburn retired 14 of 15 hitters at one point, while Mulder struck out three straight batters in three separate instances, including four straight spanning the seventh and eighth innings.

Mulder's strikeout totals were all the more remarkable against the Angels, who have struck out more than 100 fewer times than any team in the majors.

"When the game is close, it helps me stay focused," Mulder said. "I like pitching these games. It's a lot of fun."

Mulder allowed more hard-hit balls than Washburn, but the A's ace got good fielding from his teammates.

The Angels opened the third inning with two hits, but shortstop Miguel Tejada threw out Bengie Molina at home plate to help Mulder escape the jam. In the sixth, Mulder got Garret Anderson to ground into a double play with two runners on.

GARRET ANDERSON • LEFT FIELD

BY JOHN NADEL, AP SPORTS WRITER

There's a minimum of flash to Garret Anderson's game, and that's probably why he's played in virtual anonymity throughout his eight-year career with the Anaheim Angels.

"It's fine, I don't have a problem with it. It's not a bad thing," the 30-year-old left fielder said with a slight smile when asked about his newfound recognition. "I'm going about it my way."

That involves quietly going about his business on the field. He doesn't flip his bat after he hits a homer, pump his fists as he rounds the bases or leap with joy after a great catch.

"I'm not a flashy person; it's just not me," Anderson said. "I was raised to go out and play hard, let your numbers do the talking.

"I'm not worried about individual stuff. I had great numbers last year, and we didn't do well. Ultimately, it's a team thing. In professional sports, when you're winning, everybody notices you."

"It would be an understatement just to say he's been a keystone," Angels manager Mike Scioscia said. "You know he's going to get a good at-bat just about every time he's up.

Anderson shies away from such talk.

"There are a lot of reasons we're doing well," he said. "I'm not carrying this team on my back by any means."

Oakland manager Art Howe poked a little fun at the media when asked about Anderson.

"What impressed me about Garret Anderson is that nobody seems to know about him. You guys do a lousy job of promoting this guy," Howe said. "He's one of the better players in the league ever since I've been in it. This guy can flat-out hit."

And he keeps getting better.

"I've searched for ways to improve my total game," he said. "I try to be smarter about the game. What I try to do is watch the other top players, find out what they're doing.

"I'm a student of the game. I think all great players are. You can't just use your talent, you have to be thinking out on the field."

Anderson's teammates seem almost in awe.

"If there's a perfect swing, he has it," outfielder Darin Erstad said.

Troy Percival called Anderson the perfect teammate.

"He really hasn't gotten the respect he deserves," Percival said. "He's been probably the most consistent player this organization's ever had. The guy goes out there to win every day.

"Very rarely do you ever see a smile, but it's fun when you do. He'll hit that game-winning home run and then you see a smile on him and you know, hey, he did something really good today."

ANGELS CLINCH PLAYOFF BERTH, IT'S PARTY TIME

LAST POSTSEASON APPEARANCE WAS IN 1986

BY STEPHEN HAWKINS, AP SPORTS WRITER

Now, the Anaheim Angels can celebrate.

After 16 years and a four-game losing streak that kept putting off the party, the Angels finally clinched a playoff berth with a 10-5 victory over the Texas Rangers.

"We would have taken it anyway, but to have an opportunity to get to do this right here, it's pretty special," said center fielder Darin Erstad, who was

doused in champagne and beer just like everyone else in the Anaheim clubhouse.

Since their last postseason appearance in 1986, the closest the Angels got to the playoffs was when they finished a game behind Seattle in 1995, when Garret Anderson and Troy Percival were rookies.

"I had a glimpse of it my first year, but that has been a sour note in my career until now," Anderson said. "I was so close, then the last six or seven years I got a rude awakening of how hard it is to really get to the postseason. I'm enjoying this."

With the score 2-2 in the fifth, 11th-year outfielder Tim Salmon hit an RBI infield single and Anderson added a three-run homer off Colby Lewis (1-3).

Salmon and Scott Spiezio each hit a two-run homer in the seventh.

Rookie John Lackey (9-4) allowed three runs and seven hits in five-plus innings. He left after giving up consecutive singles to start the sixth.

Anaheim, which eliminated Seattle with the victory, will open the postseason as the AL wild card Tuesday in New York against the Yankees. Oakland and Minnesota have also clinched AL playoff berths.

The Angels, who had lost four straight and seven of nine, clinched on the road for the first time. The team also went to the playoffs in 1979 and 1982 but has never won a postseason series.

While Anaheim struggled the past week, the Mariners remained in contention with consecutive come-from-behind wins over the A's. But Oakland beat Seattle 5-3 in 10 innings Thursday.

"It's been a long grind. It's been emotionally draining and physically draining," Angels manager Mike Scioscia said. "We got over that little rough spot of maybe guys were trying to bull themselves through that last game to get at least to the playoffs."

Since Anaheim last played in the postseason, 25 of the other 29 major league teams had been to the playoffs.

FINAL

ANAHEIM ANGELS 10, AT TEXAS RANGERS 5

ANAHEIM	AB	R	H	RBI
D. Eckstein SS	4	1	0	0
D. Erstad CF	3	2	1	0
T. Salmon RF	4	2	2	3
A. Ochoa RF	1	0	0	0
G. Anderson LF	4	2	1	3
B. Fullmer DH	4	0	1	1
T. Glaus 3B	4	1	0	1
S. Spiezio 1B	3	1	1	2
B. Molina C	4	0	0	0
A. Kennedy 2B	4	1	2	0
Totals	35	10	8	10

HR-G. Anderson, T. Salmon, S. Spiezio

TEXAS	AB	R	H	RBI
M. Young 2B	5	0	1	0
M. Lamb LF-RF	5	1	2	1
A. Rodriguez SS	3	0	0	0
J. Hart LF	1	0	0	0
R. Palmeiro DH	4	1	1	0
H. Perry 1B	5	1	2	1
T. Hollandsworth RF	1	0	0	0
K. Mench RF-CF	4	1	1	0
T. Greene C	4	1	3	1
H. Blalock 3B	3	0	1	1
R. Rivera CF	2	0	0	0
a-T. Hafner PH	1	0	0	0
D. Sadler CF-SS	0	0	0	1
Totals	38	5	11	5

HR-T. Greene, H. Perry, M. Lamb

a-Grounded to second for R. Rivera in the 6th

Anaheim	000	240	400	—10
Texas	010	101	011	—5

Anaheim	IP	H	R	ER	BB	SO	HR	ERA
J. Lackey W	5	7	3	3	1	4	2	3.66
B. Donnelly	1	1	0	0	0	1	0	2.22
B. Weber	2	2	1	1	1	1	0	2.54
T. Percival	1	1	1	1	1	2	1	1.79

Texas	IP	H	R	ER	BB	SO	HR	ERA
C. Lewis L	4 1/3	5	6	4	4	4	1	6.29
T. Van Poppel	1 2/3	1	2	2	1	1	1	5.6
J. Alvarez	1	1	2	2	1	0	1	4.35
D. Kolb	1	1	0	0	0	0	0	3.77
A. Myette	1	0	0	0	0	1	0	10.06

J. Lackey pitched to 2 batters in the 6th

After the first three weeks this season, the Angels were 6-14—their worst 20-game start ever—and 10 1/2 games behind Seattle in the AL West. Now they have a club-record 97 wins, including 45 on the road.

Todd Greene's ninth homer gave Texas a 1-0 lead in the second, but Anaheim scored a pair of unearned runs in the fourth after an error by left fielder Mike Lamb. Brad Fullmer had an RBI double and Troy Glaus' groundout brought home another run.

The lead lasted just one pitch in the bottom half, as Herbert Perry homered. But the Angels charged right back in front in the fifth.

"I felt like I threw the ball well, and I thought the pitch to Anderson was pretty good," Lewis said. "When he hit it, I didn't think it was going to carry. That was pretty much the turning point."

"THIS MAKES EVERYTHING I'VE EVER LIVED FOR WORTH IT. IT'S THE BEST FEELING I'VE EVER HAD."

—TROY PERCIVAL

Texas rookie Hank Blalock had an RBI single in the sixth that made it 6-3. Lamb opened the ninth with a homer off Percival, who closed out the clincher nine days after his last appearance.

"I had the worst possible scenario. I had rust and too much adrenaline, but it worked out," Percival said. "I have a lot of ghosts coming out right now—Gary DiSarcina, Chuck Finley, guys who put a lot of heart in this uniform and didn't get a chance to do it here.

"This makes everything I've ever lived for worth it," he said. "It's the best feeling I've ever had."

"IT'S BEEN A LONG GRIND. IT'S BEEN EMOTIONALLY DRAINING AND PHYSICALLY DRAINING."

—MIKE SCIOSCIA

PERCIVAL A NO-SHOW IN ANGELS' SERIES-OPENING LOSS

BY JOHN NADEL, AP SPORTS WRITER

Where was Troy Percival?

With Anaheim's closer warming up in the bullpen, Scott Schoeneweis gave up a two-out, game-tying single to Jason Giambi in the eighth inning.

Bernie Williams followed with three-run homer off Brendan Donnelly to give the New York Yankees an 8-5 victory over the Angels in the opener of the AL division series.

Giambi has struck out five times and walked once in six lifetime appearances against the hard-throwing Percival, a right-hander, but Angels manager Mike Scioscia opted to go with the left-handed Schoeneweis to face Giambi, a left-handed batter.

"I've been doing this too long to get frustrated," Percival said. "I get loose, when Mike calls, I come into the game. I come in the game when they ask me to. The guys usually do such a great job."

"I don't mind Schoeney against Giambi," Scioscia said. "I think he's done a good job in the times he's faced Jason. He made a good pitch. Jason's strong. He didn't get all of it but he got enough of it to hit it by Spiez."

Giambi, who homered and singled earlier off starter Jarrod Washburn—another lefty—hit a liner off first baseman Scott Spiezio's glove and Alfonso Soriano scored easily from second as the ball bounced into short right center.

Williams then hit a 2-2 pitch from Donnelly into the right field seats for the Yankees' fourth homer of the game.

Said Schoeneweis: "He's a great hitter: I made some good pitches throughout the at-bat. He was able to put the ball in play. It's a tough play, it was just well-placed. He was able to fight it off, I tip my cap to him."

It appeared the Angels were on their way to victory behind seven strong innings by Washburn and two solo homers by Troy Glaus—the second in the eighth to put the Angels up 5-4.

Ben Weber relieved Washburn to begin the bottom of the inning and retired the first two batters before Soriano walked and stole second. Derek Jeter then walked and Scioscia opted for Schoeneweis—not Percival.

And the Yankees, winners of four of the last six World Series, took advantage.

FINAL

ANAHEIM ANGELS 5, AT NY YANKEES 8

ANAHEIM	AB	R	H	RBI
D. Eckstein SS	5	1	2	0
D. Erstad CF	4	1	3	0
T. Salmon RF	4	0	1	1
G. Anderson LF	5	0	2	2
B. Fullmer DH	4	0	0	0
T. Glaus 3B	4	2	2	2
S. Spiezio 1B	3	0	0	0
B. Molina C	4	0	1	0
A. Kennedy 2B	3	1	1	0
Totals	36	5	12	5

HR-T. Glaus 2

NY Yankees	AB	R	H	RBI
A. Soriano 2B	3	1	0	0
D. Jeter SS	2	3	2	1
J. Giambi 1B	4	2	3	3
B. Williams CF	4	1	2	3
J. Posada C	4	0	0	0
R. Mondesi RF	3	0	0	0
R. Ventura 3B	3	0	0	0
R. White DH	3	1	1	1
J. Rivera LF	1	0	0	0
a-J. Vander Wal PH	1	0	0	0
S. Spencer LF	0	0	0	0
Totals	28	8	8	8

HR-D. Jeter, J. Giambi, R. White, B. Williams

a-Lined out to left for J. Rivera in the 8th

Anaheim	001	021	010	—5
NY Yankees	100	210	04x	—8

Anaheim	IP	H	R	ER	BB	SO	HR	ERA
J. Washburn	7	6	4	4	2	2	3	5.14
B. Weber L	2/3	0	2	2	2	0	0	27
S. Schoeneweis	0	1	1	1	0	0	0	—
B. Donnelly	1/3	1	1	1	0	0	1	27

NY Yankees	IP	H	R	ER	BB	SO	HR	ERA
R. Clemens	5 2/3	8	4	4	3	5	1	6.35
R. Mendoza	1 1/3	3	1	1	0	0	1	6.75
S. Karsay W	1	0	0	0	0	1	0	0
M. Rivera S	1	1	0	0	0	0	0	0

R. Mendoza pitched to 1 batter in the 8th. S. Schoeneweis pitched to 1 batter in the 8th.

"[WILLIAMS] IS A GREAT HITTER: I MADE SOME GOOD PITCHES THROUGHOUT THE AT-BAT. HE WAS ABLE TO PUT THE BALL IN PLAY. ... I TIP MY CAP TO HIM."

—SCOTT SCHOENEWEIS

ANGELS TAKE PAGE FROM YANKEES' PLAYBOOK TO TIE SERIES

BY RONALD BLUM, AP SPORTS WRITER

Dramatic home runs. Clutch pitching by closers. Yet another late-night comeback in the Bronx.

Yes, the Anaheim Angels certainly have learned from the New York Yankees.

Garret Anderson hit a tying home run off Orlando Hernandez in the eighth inning, Troy Glaus followed with a go-ahead shot and the Angels evened their best-of-five AL playoff series by winning 8-6 in Game 2.

After watching the Yankees claw back from a 4-0 deficit to take a 5-4 lead, the crowd was stunned. It was the first time New York lost a postseason game at Yankee Stadium when leading after the seventh inning, according to the Elias Sports Bureau.

A night after not bringing in Percival and watching his bullpen squander a lead in the opener, Angels manager Mike Scioscia called for his closer with Anaheim trying to protect a 7-5 edge in the eighth.

Percival got out of the jam, throwing a called third strike past Derek Jeter, who questioned the call, with the bases loaded.

Scott Spiezio provided a cushion with a run-scoring double in the ninth off Jeff Weaver, his third hit and RBI.

The Yankees tried for one more comeback in the bottom of the ninth, with Jorge Posada blooping an RBI single with one out. But with two runners on, Percival struck out Nick Johnson and retired Raul Mondesi on a popup.

"We've got a big challenge ahead of us, no doubt about it," Scioscia said. "We've got to go out there and continue to press these guys."

Early homers by Tim Salmon and Spiezio helped Anaheim build a 4-0 lead and knock out Andy Pettitte after three innings.

El Duque, relegated to the bullpen because of the Yankees' pitching depth, replaced Pettitte in the fourth. He retired his first 11 batters and 12 of 13, but Anderson tied it when he led off the eighth with a drive into the right field bleachers. Torre elected to stay with El Duque rather than go to his regular relievers, and Glaus followed with his third homer of the series.

Unlike Tuesday, Anaheim's bullpen held on.

FINAL

ANAHEIM ANGELS 8, AT NY YANKEES 6

ANAHEIM	AB	R	H	RBI	NY YANKEES	AB	R	H	RBI
D. Eckstein SS	5	0	1	0	A. Soriano 2B	4	1	1	2
D. Erstad CF	5	0	1	0	D. Jeter SS	5	1	3	1
T. Salmon RF	5	1	1	1	J. Giambi DH	3	1	1	0
A. Ochoa RF	0	0	0	0	B. Williams CF	5	0	0	0
G. Anderson LF	5	3	3	1	R. Ventura 3B	5	1	2	0
T. Glaus 3B	5	1	2	1	J. Posada C	5	0	1	1
S. Spiezio 1B	5	1	3	3	E. Wilson PR	0	0	0	0
S. Wooten DH	4	1	3	0	N. Johnson 1B	4	1	1	0
C. Figgins PR	0	1	0	0	R. Mondesi RF	4	0	2	0
b-B. Fullmer PH	0	0	0	0	J. Rivera LF	3	1	1	2
B. Molina C	5	0	2	0	c-J. Vander Wal PH-LF	1	0	0	0
B. Gil 2B	2	0	1	1	Totals	39	6	12	6
a-A. Kennedy PH-2B	1	0	0	1					
Totals	42	8	17	8	HR-D. Jeter, A. Soriano				

HR-T. Salmon, S. Spiezio, G. Anderson, T. Glaus
a-Struck out swinging for B. Gil in the 7th
b-Intentionally walked for C. Figgins in the 9th
c-Struck out looking for J. Rivera in the 8th

Anaheim	121	000	031	—8
NY Yankees	001	202	001	—6

Anaheim	IP	H	R	ER	BB	SO	HR	ERA
K. Appier	5	5	3	3	3	3	1	5.4
F. Rodriguez W	2	2	2	2	0	1	1	9
B. Weber	1/3	2	0	0	0	0	0	18
B. Donnelly	1/3	0	0	0	0	1	0	13.5
T. Percival S	1 1/3	3	1	1	0	3	0	6.75

NY Yankees	IP	H	R	ER	BB	SO	HR	ERA
A. Pettitte	3	8	4	4	0	1	2	12
O. Hernandez L	4	3	2	2	0	4	2	4.5
S. Karsay	1/3	2	1	1	0	0	0	6.75
M. Stanton	2/3	1	0	0	0	0	0	0
J. Weaver	1	3	1	1	1	0	0	9.00

O. Hernandez pitched to 2 batters in the 8th

"WE'VE GOT A BIG CHALLENGE AHEAD OF US, NO DOUBT ABOUT IT. WE'VE GOT TO GO OUT THERE AND CONTINUE TO PRESS THESE GUYS."

—MIKE SCIOSCIA

ANGELS' BULLPEN COOLS YANKEE BATS

BY JOHN NADEL, AP SPORTS WRITER

One more win. That's all the Anaheim Angels need to reach unknown territory.

Considering the opposition, not to mention franchise history, the Angels know it won't come easy.

"This is no time to sit back and enjoy it until you clinch it," manager Mike Scioscia said after the Angels rallied from a five-run deficit to beat the New York Yankees 9-6 for a 2-1 lead in the AL division series.

"We've put ourselves in position to close it out," said Darin Erstad, who drove in the go-ahead run with a one-out double in the eighth. "We'll see what happens."

If the Angels prevail, it will mean triumph for one of the least successful franchises in baseball history over the most successful.

"I don't know what else they can do to surprise us," New York's Derek Jeter said.

The Angels' pitching did a great job of holding the

Yankees after they scored six runs off Ramon Ortiz in the first three innings.

New York had only two base runners after that, and John Lackey, Scott Schoeneweis, Francisco Rodriguez and Troy Percival teamed up to retire the last 12 batters.

"It wouldn't have been possible if not for our bullpen," Scioscia said.

Rodriguez, a 20-year-old rookie right-hander, retired the Yankees in order in the seventh and eighth, striking out four, before Percival pitched a perfect ninth.

Tim Salmon began the comeback with a two-run double off Mike Mussina in the third and completed the scoring by hitting a two-run homer on the first pitch from Steve Karsay after Erstad's double off Stanton.

Scott Spiezio's soft looper off Stanton just over the outstretched glove of second baseman Alfonso Soriano with two outs in the seventh drove in the tying run.

Kennedy began the Angels' eighth with a blooper that bounced out of right fielder Raul Mondesi's glove for a double. After David Eckstein sacrificed, Erstad lined a 1-2 pitch over first baseman Jason Giambi's head for his first RBI of the series, bringing the sellout crowd of 45,072 at Edison Field to its feet.

FINAL
NY YANKEES 6, AT ANAHEIM ANGELS 9

NY YANKEES	AB	R	H	RBI	ANAHEIM	AB	R	H	RBI
A. Soriano 2B	5	0	0	0	D. Eckstein SS	3	0	0	0
D. Jeter SS	5	1	1	0	D. Erstad CF	5	2	2	1
J. Giambi 1B	3	2	0	0	T. Salmon RF	5	1	2	4
B. Williams CF	2	2	1	0	A. Ochoa RF	0	0	0	0
R. Ventura 3B	3	0	1	3	G. Anderson LF	4	1	1	0
J. Posada C	3	0	0	1	T. Glaus 3B	3	1	1	0
R. Mondesi RF	2	1	0	0	B. Fullmer DH	3	1	2	0
N. Johnson DH	4	0	1	1	a-S. Wooten PH-DH	1	0	0	0
J. Rivera LF	4	0	2	1	S. Spiezio 1B	3	0	1	2
Totals	31	6	6	6	B. Molina C	3	0	0	0
					A. Kennedy 2B	3	3	3	2
					Totals	33	9	12	9

HR-A. Kennedy, T. Salmon

a-Flied out to shallow right-center for B. Fullmer in the 7th

NY Yankees	303 000 000	—6
Anaheim	012 101 13x	—9

NY Yankees	IP	H	R	ER	BB	SO	HR	ERA
M. Mussina	4	6	4	4	0	2	1	9
J. Weaver	1 2/3	1	1	1	2	1	0	6.75
M. Stanton L	1 2/3	4	3	3	1	1	0	11.57
S. Karsay	2/3	1	1	1	0	0	1	9

Anaheim	IP	H	R	ER	BB	SO	HR	ERA
R. Ortiz	2 2/3	3	6	6	4	1	0	20.25
J. Lackey	3	3	0	0	1	3	0	0
S. Schoeneweis	1/3	0	0	0	0	0	0	27
F. Rodriguez W	2	0	0	0	0	4	0	4.5
T. Percival S	1	0	0	0	0	0	0	3.86

"I DON'T KNOW WHAT ELSE THEY CAN DO TO SURPRISE US."

—DEREK JETER

WOOTEN, MOLINA AND GIL LEAD ANGELS PAST NEW YORK YANKEES

BY JOHN NADEL, AP SPORTS WRITER

Wooten, Molina and Gil.

How's that for a modern-day Murderers' Row?

Actually, those were the final three batters in the Anaheim Angels' lineup that beat up the New York Yankees 9-5 to end the startling AL division series.

Shawn Wooten, Bengie Molina and Benji Gil went a combined 7 for 10 with four runs scored and four RBIs as the Angels ended the Yankees' season with another shocking offensive display against New York's vaunted pitching staff.

"They brought out the whupping stick," said New York's David Wells, who entered with an 8-1 postseason record but was pounded for 10 hits and eight runs in 4 2/3 innings. "There was not much we could do."

Wooten, 6 for 9 in the series, and Gil, 4 for 5, are right-handed batters who play against some left-handed pitchers.

That's pretty good production for platoon players.

When they don't play, Brad Fullmer (2 for 7) and

Adam Kennedy (4 for 8) do, meaning the designated hitter and second base positions combined to go 16 for 29 against the Yankees.

The no-name Angels set a postseason series record by batting .376 in winning the best-of-five series 3-1, ensuring the Yankees won't be one of the participants in the World Series for the first time since 1997.

The starting rotation of Roger Clemens, Andy Pettitte, Mike Mussina and Wells combined to pitch 17 1/3 innings, allowing 32 hits and 20 earned runs for a 10.38 ERA.

So much for the old adage that good pitching stops good hitting. The Angels finished with 56 hits and 31 runs in the four games. They had 10 hits and eight runs in the fifth inning of Game 4 to take a 9-2 lead.

"Nobody wanted to make the last out," said Wooten, who homered and singled in the inning. "Next thing you knew, it was eight runs later."

"If they keep playing the way they're playing, no one is going to beat them," New York's Derek Jeter said.

FINAL

NY YANKEES 5, AT ANAHEIM ANGELS 9

NY YANKEES	AB	R	H	RBI	ANAHEIM	AB	R	H	RBI
A. Soriano 2B	5	0	1	0	D. Eckstein SS	5	1	2	1
D. Jeter SS	4	1	2	1	D. Erstad CF	5	1	2	1
J. Giambi 1B	4	0	1	0	T. Salmon RF	5	1	1	1
B. Williams CF	4	1	2	0	A. Ochoa RF	0	0	0	0
J. Posada C	5	2	3	1	G. Anderson LF	4	1	1	1
R. Mondesi RF	3	0	1	1	T. Glaus 3B	4	0	0	0
R. Coomer DH	2	0	1	0	S. Spiezio 1B	4	1	2	1
a-N. Johnson PH-DH	3	0	0	0	S. Wooten DH	4	3	3	2
R. Ventura 3B	3	0	1	1	B. Molina C	3	0	1	2
J. Rivera LF	4	1	0	0	B. Gil 2B	3	1	3	0
Totals	37	5	12	4	a-A. Kennedy PH-2B	1	0	0	0
					Totals	38	9	15	9

HR-J. Posada

HR-S. Wooten

a-Struck out swinging for R. Coomer in the 6th

a-Flied out to left for B. Gil in the 8th

NY Yankees	010	011	101	—5		
Anaheim	001	080	00x	—9		

NY Yankees	IP	H	R	ER	BB	SO	HR	ERA
D. Wells L	4 2/3	10	8	8	0	0	1	15.43
R. Mendoza	0	2	1	1	0	0	0	13.5
O. Hernandez	2 1/3	2	0	0	0	3	0	2.84
S. Karsay	2/3	0	0	0	0	0	0	6.75
M. Stanton	1/3	1	0	0	0	0	0	10.12

Anaheim	IP	H	R	ER	BB	SO	HR	ERA
J. Washburn W	5	6	2	1	1	2	0	3.75
B. Donnelly	1 1/3	2	2	2	1	1	1	13.5
S. Schoeneweis	0	1	0	0	0	0	0	27
F. Rodriguez	1 2/3	0	0	0	2	3	0	3.18
T. Percival	1	3	1	1	0	1	0	5.4

TOO MUCH MAYS FOR ANGELS AS TWINS TAKE OPENER

BY JOHN NADEL, AP SPORTS WRITER

Two days off, and suddenly the Anaheim Angels stopped hitting. They don't expect their one-game slump to last long.

After battering the New York Yankees, the Angels returned to earth with a resounding thud in a 2-1 loss to the Minnesota Twins in Game 1 of the ALCS.

The Angels couldn't do a thing against Minnesota's Joe Mays, especially after the third inning when they scored their only run on an error by shortstop Cristian Guzman.

"We're disappointed in ourselves, but you've got to give credit to Joe Mays," David Eckstein said. "He threw a dominant game."

The Angels mustered only four singles in eight innings against Mays and one against Eddie Guardado, who pitched a hitless ninth.

Adam Kennedy and Eckstein hit two-out singles in the third before Guzman booted Darin Erstad's easy grounder, allowing Kennedy to score.

After Brad Fullmer's two-out single in the fourth, Mays and Guardado combined to retire 14 straight batters until Tim Salmon walked with one out in the ninth.

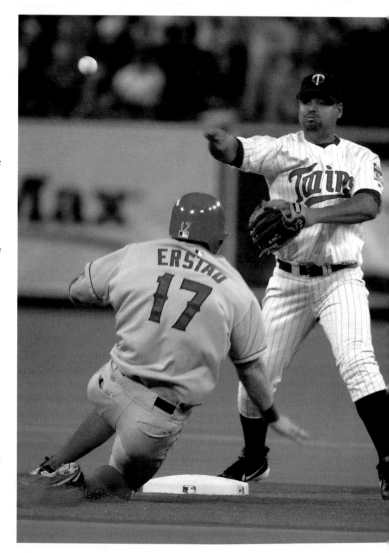

But Garret Anderson flied out and Troy Glaus struck out looking to end the game.

"I never felt like I got any pitches I wanted to take swings at," Salmon said. "Every once in a while, you run into a guy who throws a game like that. The guy threw a great game."

Salmon, Anderson and Glaus, the Angels' 3-4-5 hitters, combined to go hitless in 11 at-bats. The trio went 17 for 53 with six homers and 14 RBIs against the Yankees.

"You get used to those guys producing so much, it's a surprise when that happens," Kennedy said. "I wouldn't count on that happening for too long. We just didn't pressure them tonight. No extra-base hits, no pressure."

"We've done so well all season separating every day. Today's over. It's 1-0, they've got an advantage. It's a seven-game series. We'll come back out tomorrow ready to play."

Fullmer said the fact that the Angels haven't played in a few days as well as getting used to hitting in the Metrodome might have contributed. But he quickly added: "That kind of performance can shut down on offense. We come back tomorrow and try to get one win here."

"TODAY'S OVER. IT'S 1-0, THEY'VE GOT AN ADVANTAGE. IT'S A SEVEN-GAME SERIES. WE'LL COME BACK OUT TOMORROW READY TO PLAY."

—ADAM KENNEDY

FINAL

ANAHEIM ANGELS 1, AT MINNESOTA TWINS 2

ANAHEIM	AB	R	H	RBI
D. Eckstein SS	4	0	1	0
D. Erstad CF	4	0	1	0
T. Salmon RF	3	0	0	0
C. Figgins PR	0	0	0	0
G. Anderson LF	4	0	0	0
T. Glaus 3B	4	0	0	0
B. Fullmer DH	3	0	1	0
S. Spiezio 1B	3	0	0	0
B. Molina C	2	0	0	0
a-O. Palmeiro PH	1	0	0	0
J. Molina C	0	0	0	0
A. Kennedy 2B	3	1	1	0
Totals	31	1	4	0

MINNESOTA	AB	R	H	RBI
J. Jones LF	4	0	0	0
C. Guzman SS	3	0	1	0
C. Koskie 3B	4	0	2	1
D. Ortiz DH	3	0	1	0
b-B. Kielty PH	1	0	0	0
T. Hunter CF	3	1	1	0
D. Mientkiewicz 1B	3	0	0	0
M. Cuddyer RF	2	0	0	0
D. Mohr RF	0	0	0	0
A. Pierzynski C	2	0	0	1
L. Rivas 2B	2	1	0	0
Totals	27	2	5	2

a-Struck out swinging for B. Molina in the 8th

b-Flied out to right for D. Ortiz in the 8th

Anaheim	001	000	000	—1
Minnesota	010	010	00x	—2

Anaheim	IP	H	R	ER	BB	SO	HR	ERA
K. Appier L	5	5	2	2	3	2	0	4.5
B. Donnelly	1 2/3	0	0	0	0	2	0	7.36
S. Schoeneweis	2/3	0	0	0	0	0	0	9
B. Weber	2/3	0	0	0	0	2	0	10.8

Minnesota	IP	H	R	ER	BB	SO	HR	ERA
J. Mays W	8	4	1	0	0	3	0	4.63
E. Guardado S	1	0	0	0	1	2	0	9

American League Championship Series Game 2
Angels 6, **Twins 3** at The Metrodome

ERSTAD, FULLMER ROCK REED AS ANGELS EVEN SERIES

ASSOCIATED PRESS

So much for Minnesota's Metrodome dominance.

Darin Erstad and Brad Fullmer homered off Rick Reed as Anaheim built a six-run lead, and the high-flying Angels beat the Twins 6-3 for a split in the first two games of the ALCS.

The Angels got to Reed from the start. Erstad, the No. 2 batter, sent Reed's sixth pitch over the fence in right center, where it landed 409 feet away—nestled in one of the stacked-up seats used for Vikings games.

"It's nice to get a lead. It's nice to jump out. That gave us a big lift," Angels manager Mike Scioscia said.

When Fullmer chased Reed with a two-run homer in the sixth, it seemed over. But Minnesota battled right back, knocking Ramon Ortiz out in the sixth when Corey Koskie hit an RBI single and Doug Mientkiewicz, who had three hits, had a two-run single.

Brendan Donnelly replaced Ortiz and got out of the inning, and 20-year-old rookie Francisco Rodriguez struck out two in a 1-2-3 seventh.

After a two-out walk to Torii Hunter and a single by Mientkiewicz put runners at the corners in the eighth, Scioscia brought in Troy Percival. "Percy is a guy we do have available for four outs when necessary," said Scioscia, who brought in his closer just four times in the eighth during the regular season.

Percival got ahead 1-2 in the count on pinch hitter Bobby Kielty. With the crowd on its feet, shouting and waving Homer Hankies, Kielty took a called third strike on a change-up.

"It came back nice over the inside corner," said Percival, who finished up with a perfect ninth for the save. He struck out three of the four batters he faced.

"Our job was to come here and win one out of two on the road," Fullmer said.

Erstad put the Angels ahead in the first with his first postseason homer.

After failing to get a leadoff hitter on in the first 10 innings of the series, Anaheim's first three batters got hits in the second, with Scott Spiezio's bloop double near the right field line bouncing over an onrushing Michael Cuddyer to make it 2-0.

Reed caught Adam Kennedy leaning and threw to first for the pickoff. Kennedy broke for second, Spiezio then headed home from third, and Mientkiewicz threw to the plate. But Pierzynski couldn't handle the throw as Spiezio made contact with him and scored. David Eckstein's RBI single made it 4-0.

Ortiz allowed three runs and 10 hits in 5 1/3 innings, repeatedly pitching out of trouble.

FINAL

ANAHEIM ANGELS 6, AT MINNESOTA TWINS 3

ANAHEIM	AB	R	H	RBI	MINNESOTA	AB	R	H	RBI
D. Eckstein SS	5	0	2	1	J. Jones LF	5	0	0	0
D. Erstad CF	5	1	2	1	C. Guzman SS	4	1	2	0
T. Salmon RF	2	0	0	0	C. Koskie 3B	3	1	1	1
O. Palmeiro RF	1	0	0	0	D. Ortiz DH	4	0	1	0
a-A. Ochoa PH-RF	2	0	0	0	T. Hunter CF	3	1	1	0
G. Anderson LF	4	0	0	0	D. Mientkiewicz 1B	4	0	3	2
T. Glaus 3B	3	2	2	0	M. Cuddyer RF	3	0	1	0
B. Fullmer DH	3	1	2	2	c-B. Kielty PH-RF	1	0	0	0
b-S. Wooten PH	1	0	0	0	A. Pierzynski C	4	0	1	0
S. Spiezio 1B	4	1	2	1	L. Rivas 2B	3	0	1	0
B. Molina C	4	0	0	0	d-D. Mohr PH	1	0	0	0
A. Kennedy 2B	4	1	0	0	Totals	35	3	11	3
Totals	38	6	10	5					

HR-D. Erstad, B. Fullmer

a-Struck out swinging for O. Palmeiro in the 7th
b-Struck out swinging for B. Fullmer in the 8th
c-Struck out looking for M. Cuddyer in the 8th
d-Struck out swinging for L. Rivas in the 9th

Anaheim	130	002	000	—6
Minnesota	000	003	000	—3

Anaheim	IP	H	R	ER	BB	SO	HR	ERA
R. Ortiz W	5 1/3	10	3	3	1	3	0	10.12
B. Donnelly	2/3	0	0	0	0	1	0	6.23
F. Rodriguez	1 2/3	1	0	0	1	3	0	2.45
T. Percival S	1 1/3	0	0	0	0	3	0	3.86
Minnesota	IP	H	R	ER	BB	SO	HR	ERA
R. Reed L	5 1/3	8	6	4	0	0	2	6.97
J. Santana	1 2/3	0	0	0	0	3	0	3.86
J. Romero	1/3	0	0	0	1	0	0	0
L. Hawkins	2/3	0	0	0	0	1	0	0
M. Jackson	1	2	0	0	0	2	0	0

HAPPY HOMECOMING FOR ANGELS

ASSOCIATED PRESS

The Anaheim Angels monkeyed around with Minnesota for seven innings, then watched Troy Glaus put them in control of the AL championship series.

Glaus hit a tie-breaking homer off J.C. Romero in the eighth inning, and the Angels got two great catches in the ninth to beat the Twins 2-1 to take a 2-1 series lead.

Garret Anderson's second-inning homer off Eric Milton had put the Angels ahead, and Jarrod Washburn seemed unstoppable until Jacque Jones' RBI double to left over Anderson in the seventh, which ended an 0-for-18 skid.

Anaheim failed to get a run despite advancing a runner to third with one out in the seventh, but Glaus led off the eighth with his fourth homer of the postseason, an opposite-field drive into the right field bleachers off Romero, the Twins' fifth pitcher.

Percival closed it out with a 1-2-3 ninth for his fourth save of the postseason. He got a fine diving catch from right fielder Alex Ochoa on Doug Mientkiewicz's sinking liner for the first out and a sliding catch in shallow left by Anderson on a soft fly by A.J. Pierzynski that ended the game.

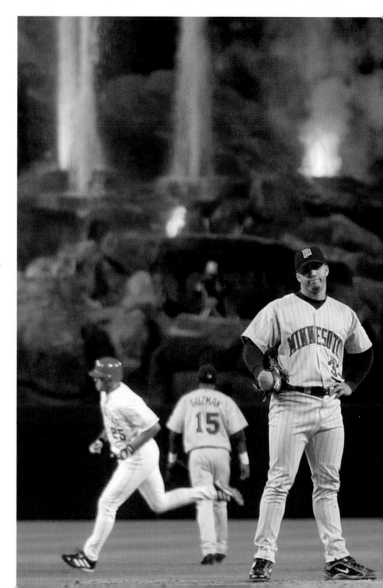

"They were both fantastic catches," Percival said. "That last one, I thought there was no chance in the world at it, because I know Garret was playing fairly deep with a lefty up covering that gap. But he comes in on the ball better than anybody I've seen in left field. I'm glad to have him out there."

Washburn was dominant. He started his first 12 batters with strikes, allowed just two leadoff batters to reach base and went to a three-ball count twice.

He gave up six hits—all singles until Jones' double—struck out seven and walked none in seven innings before turning it over to the best bullpen in baseball. Francisco Rodriguez improved to 3-0 in the postseason by striking out two in a perfect eighth.

Milton, 4-0 with a 1.50 ERA in five career starts at Anaheim coming in, was hurt only by Anderson, his least favorite Angels batter. Anderson, a .364 (8 for 22) hitter with four homers off Milton coming in, turned on a 91 mph chest-high pitch leading off the second inning, depositing it in the right field bleachers.

Anaheim nearly went ahead in the seventh when Bengie Molina walked against LaTroy Hawkins leading off. Benji Gil sacrificed and David Eckstein singled, a ball that went just off the webbing of the glove of second baseman Luis Rivas, who tried for a leaping grab.

Pinch runner Chone Figgins went to third, and Johan Santana came in to face Darin Erstad. He threw a wild pitch that bounced about 40 feet up the third base line, but Figgins held as Eckstein advanced. Erstad then grounded to Rivas, who threw out Figgins at the plate. Mike Jackson walked Salmon, loading the bases, and Anderson flied to the right field warning track against Romero.

FINAL
MINNESOTA TWINS 1, AT ANAHEIM ANGELS 2

MINNESOTA	AB	R	H	RBI
J. Jones LF	4	0	1	1
C. Guzman SS	4	0	0	0
C. Koskie 3B	4	0	0	0
M. LeCroy DH	3	0	1	0
a-D. Ortiz PH-DH	1	0	0	0
T. Hunter CF	4	0	1	0
D. Mientkiewicz 1B	4	0	0	0
D. Mohr RF	4	1	2	0
A. Pierzynski C	4	0	0	0
L. Rivas 2B	3	0	1	0
Totals	35	1	6	1

a-Struck out swinging for M. LeCroy in the 8th

ANAHEIM	AB	R	H	RBI
D. Eckstein SS	4	0	1	0
D. Erstad CF	4	0	1	0
T. Salmon RF	3	0	0	0
A. Ochoa RF	0	0	0	0
G. Anderson LF	4	1	2	1
T. Glaus 3B	3	1	2	1
S. Spiezio 1B	3	0	0	0
S. Wooten DH	4	0	1	0
B. Molina C	2	0	0	0
C. Figgins PR	0	0	0	0
J. Molina C	1	0	0	0
B. Gil 2B	2	0	0	0
Totals	30	2	7	2

HR-G. Anderson, T. Glaus

Minnesota	000	000	100	—1		
Anaheim	010	000	01x	—2		

Minnesota	IP	H	R	ER	BB	SO	HR	ERA
E. Milton	6	5	1	1	2	4	1	2.08
L. Hawkins	1/3	1	0	0	1	0	0	0
J. Santana	1/3	0	0	0	0	0	0	3.6
M. Jackson	0	0	0	0	1	0	0	0
J. Romero L	1 1/3	1	1	1	0	2	1	1.8

Anaheim	IP	H	R	ER	BB	SO	HR	ERA
J. Washburn	7	6	1	1	0	7	0	2.84
F. Rodriguez W	1	0	0	0	0	2	0	2.16
T. Percival S	1	0	0	0	0	0	0	3.18

M. Jackson pitched to 1 batter in the 7th

American League Championship Series Game 4
Angels 7, Twins 1 at Edison Field

ROOKIE LACKEY'S PITCHING PUTS ANGELS ON THE BRINK

ASSOCIATED PRESS

For 16 years, the Angels waited to get back. Now they're on the verge again, and just like in 1986, they have three tries at winning the first pennant in franchise history.

"I don't think I'll be able to sleep tonight. One more win and we're in!" Bengie Molina said after Anaheim broke up a scoreless game in the seventh inning and beat the Minnesota Twins 7-1 for a 3-1 lead in the ALCS.

Rookie John Lackey outpitched Brad Radke with seven shutout innings, postseason star Troy Glaus hit a go-ahead single in the seventh and Anaheim broke it open against Minnesota's bullpen.

And it happened exactly 16 years to the day that the Angels were just one strike from a World Series trip before Boston's Dave Henderson homered off Donnie Moore, starting the Angels' downward spiral. The Red Sox came back to win in extra innings, then won the next two games at Fenway Park to win the series 4-3.

"We're not counting anything yet. There's a huge challenge ahead of us," Angels manager Mike Scioscia said

"For a youngster who was in the minor leagues three months ago to come up and do that was incredible,"

Scioscia said. "John was about as on tonight as you could be."

Lackey's only previous postseason appearance was in Game 3 of the first-round series against the New York Yankees, when he pitched three shutout innings in the Angels' comeback from a five-run deficit. He hadn't started since Sept. 26, but allowed just one leadoff runner, using a sharp breaking ball, and kept his fastball down to stifle the Twins.

Radke allowed just two hits in the first six innings, went to just one 2-0 count and didn't go to three balls on any batters.

"He did everything he was supposed to do for this baseball team," Twins manager Ron Gardenhire said. "Their hits were bloops. They got one solid hit–Glaus hit a solid ball."

Darin Erstad singled leading off the seventh, becoming Anaheim's third runner. When he broke for second on a steal attempt, Minnesota's defense cracked again. Catcher A.J. Pierzynski's throw bounced into center for the Twins' seventh error of the postseason, and Erstad took third.

Tim Salmon walked, Garret Anderson popped out and Glaus lined a 1-0 pitch into left field for the first run. Scott Spiezio added a bloop RBI double that landed just inside the right field line.

It got ugly in the eighth, after Erstad hit a one-out single and Johan Santana threw away a pickoff for error No. 8. Anderson singled in a run off J.C. Romero, and Mike Jackson gave up Brad Fullmer's two-run double and Molina's two-run triple–his first in two years.

Francisco Rodriguez pitched the eighth, and Ben Weber finished the six-hitter, giving up an RBI single to David Ortiz.

FINAL

MINNESOTA TWINS 1, AT ANAHEIM ANGELS 7

MINNESOTA	AB	R	H	RBI	ANAHEIM	AB	R	H	RBI
J. Jones LF	4	0	0	0	D. Eckstein SS	4	0	1	0
C. Guzman SS	4	0	0	0	D. Erstad CF	4	2	2	0
C. Koskie 3B	4	1	1	0	T. Salmon RF	2	0	0	0
D. Ortiz DH	4	0	2	1	A. Ochoa PR-RF	1	1	0	0
T. Hunter CF	4	0	0	0	G. Anderson LF	4	1	1	1
D. Mientkiewicz 1B	3	0	1	0	T. Glaus 3B	4	1	2	1
D. Mohr RF	3	0	1	0	B. Fullmer DH	4	1	1	2
A. Pierzynski C	3	0	0	0	S. Spiezio 1B	3	1	1	1
L. Rivas 2B	2	0	1	0	B. Molina C	3	0	2	2
a-B. Kielty PH	1	0	0	0	A. Kennedy 2B	3	0	0	0
D. Lamb 2B	0	0	0	0	Totals	32	7	10	7
Totals	32	1	6	1					

a-Struck out swinging for L Rivas in the 8th

Minnesota	000	000	001	—1	
Anaheim	000	000	25x	—7	

Minnesota	IP	H	R	ER	BB	SO	HR	ERA
B. Radke L	6 2/3	5	2	2	1	4	0	1.96
J. Santana	2/3	1	1	1	0	0	0	4.76
L. Hawkins	1/3	0	0	0	0	0	0	0
J. Romero	0	1	1	1	0	0	0	3.6
M. Jackson	0	3	3	3	1	0	0	16.2
B. Wells	1/3	0	0	0	0	1	0	0

Anaheim	IP	H	R	ER	BB	SO	HR	ERA
J. Lackey W	7	3	0	0	0	7	0	0
F. Rodriguez	1	1	0	0	0	2	0	1.93
B. Weber	1	2	1	1	0	1	0	10.12

J. Romero pitched to 1 batter in the 8th. M. Jackson pitched to 4 batters in the 8th.

KENNEDY'S THREE HOMERS SEND ANGELS TO THEIR FIRST WORLD SERIES

BY JOHN NADEL, AP SPORTS WRITER

With the help of Adam Kennedy's newfound power, Anaheim finally made it to the World Series, where no Angels team had gone before.

"I know Mr. Autry's smiling up there, and I'm so happy that Jackie's here to enjoy it with us," Tim Salmon said. "To be with this organization as long as I have, and to feel the emptiness of the fans all these years, and the pain and frustration, it's like we're paving a new road here."

Kennedy, a No. 9 hitter with little previous proclivity for power, had three home runs, four hits and five RBIs, the most heavenly game of his baseball career.

"This was a goal of Gene's all of his life in baseball, and the fact that he was not here to see it personally—I know he's watching it from somewhere," said his widow, Jackie, who gave the AL trophy to manager Mike Scioscia in her role as honorary league president.

Anaheim had just wasted a 3-2 lead in the sixth when Kennedy's three-run drive off Johan Santana erased a 5-3 deficit and made him just the fifth player to homer three times in a postseason game.

"They're on a roll," Twins manager Ron Gardenhire said. "Those guys, they just keep playing. And they

keep swinging. Goodness gracious, I don't know if I've ever seen an inning like that. We couldn't get anybody out. They were hitting balls through holes, over—bullets."

When David Eckstein caught the final out—just as he did in the division series—he ran over to Kennedy and tapped gloves, then danced with Salmon.

The Angels jumped on each other in a mob between first base and the mound. Fans cheered as Salmon, in his 11th Angels season and the team's senior member, ran around with the AL championship trophy. Percival joined his teammates for a lap around the field.

Hoping to send the series back to the Metrodome, the Twins took a 2-0 lead on David Ortiz's RBI double in the first and A.J. Pierzynski's run-scoring single in the second.

Kennedy, 1 for 10 in the first four games, started the comeback with a third-inning homer off Game 1 winner Joe Mays, and Spiezio's homer tied it leading off the fifth. One out later, Kennedy put the Angels ahead with a drive into the right field bleachers.

FINAL

MINNESOTA TWINS 5, AT ANAHEIM ANGELS 13

MINNESOTA	AB	R	H	RBI	ANAHEIM	AB	R	H	RBI
J. Jones LF	3	0	1	1	D. Eckstein SS	4	1	1	1
C. Guzman SS	3	0	0	0	D. Erstad CF	5	1	2	1
C. Koskie 3B	3	1	1	0	T. Salmon RF	4	0	3	0
D. Ortiz DH	4	0	1	1	A. Ochoa PR-RF	1	1	0	0
T. Hunter CF	4	0	0	0	G. Anderson LF	4	1	2	1
M. Cuddyer RF	0	0	0	0	T. Glaus 3B	5	0	0	0
D. Mientkiewicz 1B	4	1	1	0	B. Fullmer DH	2	0	0	0
D. Mohr RF-CF	4	2	2	0	b-S. Wooten PH-DH3	1	1	1	1
A. Pierzynski C	3	1	3	1	S. Spiezio 1B	4	3	3	3
T. Prince C	1	0	0	0	B. Molina C	3	0	1	0
L. Rivas 2B	2	0	0	0	C. Figgins PR	1	2	1	0
a-B. Kielty PH	0	0	0	1	J. Molina C	0	0	0	0
D. Lamb 2B	0	0	0	0	A. Kennedy 2B	4	3	4	5
Totals	31	5	9	4	Totals	40	13	18	12

a-Walked for L Rivas in the 7th
b-Struck out swinging for B Fullmer in the 6th

HR-A. Kennedy 3, S. Spiezio

Minnesota	110	000	300	—5		
Anaheim	001	020	10x	—13		

Minnesota	IP	H	R	ER	BB	SO	HR	ERA
J. Mays	5 1/3	8	3	3	0	0	3	4.76
J. Santana L	2/3	3	3	3	0	1	1	8.53
L. Hawkins	0	3	3	3	0	0	0	7.36
J. Romero	1/3	2	3	3	1	1	0	8.44
B. Wells	2/3	2	1	1	0	1	0	9
K. Lohse	1	0	0	0	0	1	0	0

Anaheim	IP	H	R	ER	BB	SO	HR	ERA
K. Appier	5 1/3	5	2	2	1	1	0	4.11
B. Donnelly	1	3	3	3	0	2	0	10.12
F. Rodriguez	W2/3	0	0	0	1	0	0	1.8
B. Weber	1	1	0	0	0	0	0	7.36
T. Percival	1	0	0	0	0	0	0	2.7

J. Santana pitched to 3 batters in the 7th. L. Hawkins pitched to 3 batters in the 7th

Francisco Rodriguez, Anaheim's 20-year-old rookie sensation, brought back memories of past failures. He walked pinch hitter Bobby Kielty in the sixth, forcing home the tying run, then threw a wild pitch that put Minnesota ahead and gave up Jacque Jones' sacrifice fly.

But the lead didn't last long, and Rodriguez wound up with yet another win. He's now 4-0 in this year's playoffs—the first four victories of his major league career.

Spiezio and Bengie Molina singled off Santana, who had escaped a two-on jam in the sixth. Kennedy bunted the first pitch foul, fouled another pitch off with a swing, then smacked a hanging curveball over the wall in right center.

World Series, Game 1
Giants 4, Angels 3 at Edison Field

ANGELS COME UP SHORT IN GAME ONE

BY JOHN NADEL, AP SPORTS WRITER

After a postseason filled with big hits, the Anaheim Angels came up short against San Francisco in Game 1 of the World Series.

The result was a 4-3 loss to the Giants.

"It just didn't happen," said Anaheim's Darin Erstad, who went 1 for 5, struck out twice and flied out against closer Robb Nen to end the game. "What do you do? We tried. We chased some pitches, including myself."

Giants starter Jason Schmidt allowed nine hits in 5 2/3 innings, but Anaheim managed only three runs off him. The capable San Francisco bullpen held the Angels hitless after that.

The Angels constantly talk about putting pressure on the opposition by using the hit-and-run or attempting to steal on a regular basis.

And they often play small-ball to perfection, moving runners up with the bunt or by hitting to the right side.

It all happened that way several times in this game.

But the big hit just wasn't there.

The Angels, who entered the World Series hitting .328 with 60 runs in nine postseason games, left a runner at second base in the second and another at third in the third.

Then, they left runners at second and third in the fourth and first and third in the fifth.

"The only things that were uncharacteristic—we had runners at third with less than two outs and didn't score," Angels manager Mike Scioscia said. "Guys on third base with less than two outs, we've been very good bringing them in.

"We did some things we needed to. A couple of at-bats, we didn't get it done. I saw a lot of positive things tonight. The score wasn't where we wanted it to be."

After Troy Glaus homered with one out in the second, Brad Fullmer singled and stole

FINAL

SAN FRANCISCO GIANTS 4, AT ANAHEIM ANGELS 3

SAN FRANCISCO	AB	R	H	RBI	ANAHEIM	AB	R	H	RBI
K. Lofton CF	3	0	0	0	D. Eckstein SS	5	0	1	0
R. Aurilia SS	4	0	0	0	D. Erstad CF	5	0	1	0
J. Kent 2B	4	0	0	0	T. Salmon RF	4	0	0	0
B. Bonds LF	3	1	1	1	G. Anderson LF	4	0	1	0
B. Santiago C	4	0	1	0	T. Glaus 3B	4	2	2	2
R. Sanders RF	3	2	2	1	B. Fullmer DH	3	1	1	0
J. Snow 1B	3	1	1	2	S. Spiezio 1B	3	0	1	0
D. Bell 3B	4	0	0	0	C. Figgins PR	0	0	0	0
T. Shinjo DH	3	0	1	0	S. Wooten 1B	0	0	0	0
a-T. Goodwin PH-DH	1	0	0	0	B. Molina C	3	0	0	0
Totals	32	4	6	4	b-O. Palmeiro PH	1	0	0	0
					J. Molina C	0	0	0	0
HR-B. Bonds, J. Snow					A. Kennedy 2B	4	0	2	1
					Totals	36	3	9	3

a-Grounded to shortstop for T. Shinjo in the 9th

b-Fouled out to third for B. Molina in the 8th

HR-T. Glaus 2

San Francisco   020   002   000   —4
Anaheim   010   002   000   —3

San Francisco	IP	H	R	ER	BB	SO	HR	ERA
J. Schmidt W	5 2/3	9	3	3	1	6	2	4.76
F. Rodriguez	1 1/3	0	0	0	0	1	0	0
T. Worrell	1	0	0	0	1	1	0	0
R. Nen S	1	0	0	0	0	1	0	0

Anaheim	IP	H	R	ER	BB	SO	HR	ERA
J. Washburn L	5 2/3	6	4	4	2	5	3	6.35
B. Donnelly	1 2/3	0	0	0	0	0	0	0
S. Schoeneweis	0	0	0	0	1	0	0	0
B. Weber	1 2/3	0	0	0	0	2	0	0

S. Schoeneweis pitched to 1 batter in the 8th

second after Scott Spiezio made the second out. But Bengie Molina flied to left.

Adam Kennedy doubled off the scoreboard in right center to open the third on the first pitch he saw since going 4 for 4 with three homers in Anaheim's ALCS-clinching 13-5 victory over Minnesota.

David Eckstein fought off an inside pitch to ground to second, advancing Kennedy to third, but Erstad struck out and Tim Salmon flied to center.

Garret Anderson singled to start the fourth and went to third on Spiezio's two-out double, but Molina grounded to third.

Eckstein singled with one out in the fifth and took third on Erstad's hit-and-run single. But Salmon fouled out when first baseman J.T. Snow jumped quickly to his feet after slipping in front of the Giants' dugout to make the catch, and Anderson struck out.

After Glaus hit his second solo homer in the sixth to trim San Francisco's lead to 4-2, Fullmer walked and one out later was running when Molina hit a grounder to third.

That forced David Bell to throw to first on what would have almost surely been a double play considering Molina's lack of speed. And it resulted in a run when Fullmer scored from second on a single by Kennedy.

The Angels didn't threaten again.

"Our game is getting runners in scoring position, getting them in," hitting coach Mickey Hatcher said. "It didn't happen for us today. We'll turn the page and come back tomorrow. I'm not worried about it. We did a good job against Schmidt."

But not with runners on base.

"We had some opportunities, he made pitches when he had to, he got out of trouble each time," Fullmer said.

"Schmidt definitely beared down, made the big pitches when he needed to," Eckstein said.

Considering how well the Angels responded to series-opening losses earlier this month, they shouldn't be discouraged.

"I'm not going to say we're right where we want to be, but we've been here before. Nobody's going to panic," Fullmer said.

"We lost, but we've got more games to play," Eckstein said.

Glaus became the 27th player to hit a homer in his first World Series at-bat just minutes after San Francisco's Barry Bonds became the 26th.

ANGELS BEAT GIANTS ON SALMON HOMER

BY BEN WALKER, AP SPORTS WRITER

Tim Salmon waited a long time for his World Series moment.

Salmon hit his second homer of the game, a tie-breaking two-run shot with two outs in the eighth inning that lifted the Anaheim Angels over the San Francisco Giants 11-10, ending a thrilling, seesaw game and evening the Series at one-all.

No active player in the majors had gone longer than Salmon—1,388 games—without reaching the postseason until this year. Yet it had been Barry Bonds' absence from the Series that had attracted all the attention—until Salmon connected off Felix Rodriguez to give the Angels their first-ever World Series win.

"I think I made the most of my opportunities. It was awesome," Salmon said. "The way the game went back and forth was unbelievable.

"We knew there was going to be a hero in the dugout," he said, "and tonight it was me."

Much of the credit belonged to Francisco Rodriguez, too. The 20-year-old rookie sensation pitched three perfect innings and got the victory, making him 5-0 in the postseason. He tied Randy Johnson's record set last year for wins in a single postseason.

Bonds homered for the second straight day, launching a solo shot with two outs in the ninth off Angels closer Troy Percival. But the crowd of 44,584 roared as Percival finished it without further damage for a save.

It was the highest scoring game in the Series since Cleveland beat Florida 14-11 in 1997.

Pacific Bell Park will host the World Series for the first time in Game 3 Tuesday night. Livan Hernandez, 6-0 lifetime in the postseason, starts for the Giants against Ramon Ortiz.

Salmon went 4 for 4 with a walk, driving in four runs and scoring three. As he circled the bases with fireworks exploded overhead after connecting on a 93 mph fastball, Felix Rodriguez angrily tugged on his cap.

The homer capped the Angels' comeback from a 9-7 deficit. They had led 5-0 after the first inning before homers rallied the Giants.

"You could tell it was going to be an offensive night," Giants manager Dusty Baker said. "The ball was carrying.

"It was one of the best games I've ever been in," he said.

"THE WAY THE GAME WENT BACK AND FORTH WAS UNBELIEVABLE."

—TIM SALMON

FINAL

SAN FRANCISCO GIANTS 10, AT ANAHEIM ANGELS 11

SAN FRANCISCO	AB	R	H	RBI	ANAHEIM	AB	R	H	RBI
K. Lofton CF	5	0	1	0	D. Eckstein SS	5	3	3	0
R. Aurilia SS	5	1	1	0	D. Erstad CF	5	2	2	1
J. Kent 2B	5	1	1	1	T. Salmon RF	4	3	4	4
B. Bonds LF	2	3	1	1	A. Ochoa RF	0	0	0	0
B. Santiago C	5	1	1	0	G. Anderson LF	5	1	2	2
J. Snow 1B	4	2	2	2	T. Glaus 3B	4	1	2	0
R. Sanders RF	4	1	2	3	B. Fullmer DH	3	1	2	1
D. Bell 3B	4	1	2	2	S. Spiezio 1B	3	0	1	2
S. Dunston DH	4	0	1	1	B. Molina C	4	0	0	0
Totals	38	10	12	10	A. Kennedy 2B	4	0	0	0
					Totals	37	11	16	10

HR-R. Sanders, D. Bell, J. Kent,
B. Bonds   HR-T. Salmon 2

San Francisco	0 4 1	0 4 0	0 0 1	—10		
Anaheim	5 2 0	0 1 1	0 2 x	—11		

San Francisco	IP	H	R	ER	BB	SO	HR	ERA
R. Ortiz	1 2/3	9	7	7	0	0	1	37.8
C. Zerbe	4	4	2	1	0	0	0	2.25
J. Witasick	0	0	0	0	1	0	0	0
A. Fultz	1/3	1	0	0	0	0	0	0
F. Rodriguez L	1 2/3	2	2	2	1	0	1	6
T. Worrell	1/3	0	0	0	0	0	0	0

Anaheim	IP	H	R	ER	BB	SO	HR	ERA
K. Appier	2	5	5	5	2	2	3	22.5
J. Lackey	2 1/3	2	2	2	1	1	0	7.71
B. Weber	2/3	4	2	2	0	1	0	7.71
F. Rodriguez W	3	0	0	0	0	4	0	0
T. Percival S	1	1	1	1	0	0	1	9

K Appier pitched to 2 batters in the 3rd. J. Witasick pitched to 1 batter in the 6th

Bonds, making his first Series appearance in his 17th major league season, went 1 for 2 with three walks. Like everyone else in the San Francisco lineup, he couldn't solve Rodriguez as he grounded out. The rookie pitcher struck out four.

A day after both bullpens pitched 3 1/3 hitless innings, most of the relievers had a lot more trouble getting outs.

The Giants scored four times in the fifth off John Lackey and Ben Weber for a 9-7 lead. Game 1 star J.T. Snow hit a tying two-run single, then hustled to avoid being forced to give David Bell a go-ahead infield hit with two outs. Shawon Dunston, playing in his first Series game at age 39, added a sharp RBI single.

Scott Spiezio's sacrifice fly off Chad Zerbe pulled the Angels within a run in the fifth.

The Rally Monkey made its first appearance on the scoreboard in the sixth. And for the second straight night, the Angels promptly scored, with Garret Anderson's single off Aaron Fultz making it 9-9.

When Brad Fullmer walked in the Anaheim seventh, that monkey mascot once again began bobbing up and down. It was hard to tell whether any of the Giants noticed, though it was a safe guess someone on their side did.

"Well, you definitely observe it," San Francisco closer Robb Nen said before the game. "You see him."

The Angels started out doing everything right—of their first 15 swings against Russ Ortiz, they did not miss once. In an inning symbolic of their whole season, they hit to the opposite field, aggressively streaked around the bases and even pulled a double steal that let Fullmer sneak home.

David Eckstein's leadoff single started the hit parade. Darin Erstad followed with an RBI double and Salmon and Anderson added singles. After Troy Glaus hit a fly ball for the first out, Fullmer and Spiezio had RBI singles.

Anaheim clearly had the Giants on the run, and took advantage. When catcher Benito Santiago made a high throw trying to get Spiezio at second, Fullmer breezed to the plate with the Series' first steal of home since Tim McCarver did it for St. Louis in 1964.

In all, it was the biggest first inning in a Series game since Baltimore scored five against Pittsburgh in the 1979 opener.

Now winless in five career postseason starts, Kevin Appier began with a good omen: Giants leadoff man Kenny Lofton was called out on strikes by a plate umpire whose first name was Angel—Angel Hernandez.

But given a big lead, Appier began to give it right back. And even though home runs eventually cost him, it was a little walk that led to his undoing.

Working too carefully, Appier walked Bonds on a close 3-2 pitch to begin the second. Snow singled with one out and Reggie Sanders launched a three-run drive to left.

Bell followed with a shot to straightaway center, closing the Giants' gap to 5-4. It marked the 13th set of back-to-back homers in Series play, with Tony Gwynn and Greg Vaughn doing it most recently for San Diego in 1998.

By then, as the bullpen got busy, it was apparent the Angels could not count on the pitcher they fondly call "Ape." Instead, they would have to warm up the Rally Monkey, too.

Salmon's two-run homer gave the Angels 7-4 in the second, an inning that started with Eckstein's bunt single. Glaus' long double chased Ortiz before he got another chance to face Fullmer, his one time high school teammate.

Jeff Kent homered to lead off the Giants' third, and Appier was pulled after a four-pitch walk to Bonds. At that point, all nine of San Francisco's runs in the Series had scored on homers.

World Series, Game 3
Angels 10, **Giants** 4 at Pacific Bell Park

ANGELS' TORRID HITTING WINS GAME THREE

BY BEN WALKER, AP SPORTS WRITER

They were relentless—at the plate, on the bases.

Scott Spiezio, Darin Erstad and the Angels trampled San Francisco 10-4, crashing the Giants' homecoming and taking a 2-1 lead in the World Series.

"I'm not going to say I'm surprised because I think if we can keep pressuring clubs the way we've been doing all year and in the playoffs, you have the potential to do something like we did tonight," Anaheim manager Mike Scioscia said.

Spiezio drove in three runs, Erstad had three hits and the Angels battered Livan Hernandez, the postseason ace who recently boasted, "I never lose in October."

The Angels became the first team in Series history to bat around in consecutive innings, with a torrent of hits, walks and steals making it 8-1 in the fourth.

"Everybody knows that one run isn't enough, two runs aren't enough," Spiezio said. "No matter how many runs we score, we're going to go up there and act like that's the biggest at-bat we've ever had."

"We're just not keeping pace with the Angels right now. We're embarrassed a little bit today, but we'll come back from it," Giants second baseman Jeff Kent said. "We always do."

The Angels finished with 16 hits in keeping up a familiar pattern. They've lost the opener in all three of their postseason series this year, then didn't lose again. After dropping Game 1 to the Giants, they came back to win 11-10.

We've been through tough times before," Erstad said. "We have it rolling right now."

"It was a tough night for us," San Francisco manager Dusty Baker said. "They were hitting. They've been hitting the last two games. I don't know, hopefully they hit themselves out, I hope."

Bonds did his best, becoming the first player to homer in his first three Series games. His 437-foot, two-run shot to center field came in the fifth, the same inning Rich Aurilia connected for the Giants, but only made it 8-4.

Bonds set a postseason record with his seventh home run and also drew two more walks.

With 13 homers already, Anaheim and San Francisco are only four short of the record for any Series. The long balls are sure to further increase speculation that juiced balls are being used, though commissioner Bud Selig insists it's not so.

FINAL

ANAHEIM ANGELS 10, AT SAN FRANCISCO GIANTS 4

ANAHEIM	AB	R	H	RBI	SAN FRANCISCO	AB	R	H	RBI
D. Eckstein SS	5	1	2	1	K. Lofton CF	4	1	0	0
D. Erstad CF	6	2	3	0	R. Aurilia SS	5	1	2	1
T. Salmon RF	4	2	1	1	J. Kent 2B	4	1	2	0
S. Schoeneweis P	0	0	0	0	B. Bonds LF	2	1	1	2
G. Anderson LF	6	0	1	1	B. Santiago C	4	0	0	1
T. Glaus 3B	5	2	2	1	J. Snow 1B	4	0	1	0
S. Spiezio 1B	5	1	2	3	R. Sanders RF	4	0	0	0
A. Kennedy 2B	5	1	2	1	D. Bell 3B	1	0	0	0
B. Molina C	2	1	2	1	L. Hernandez P	0	0	0	0
R. Ortiz P	3	0	0	0	J. Witasick P	0	0	0	0
a-S. Wooten PH	1	0	0	0	c-P. Feliz PH	1	0	0	0
B. Donnelly P	0	0	0	0	A. Fultz P	0	0	0	0
b-B. Gil PH	1	0	1	0	d-S. Dunston PH	1	0	0	0
A. Ochoa RF	0	0	0	0	F. Rodriguez P	0	0	0	0
Totals	43	10	16	9	S. Eyre P	0	0	0	0
					e- R. Martinez PH	1	0	0	0
					Totals	31	4	6	4

a-Fouled out to first for R. Ortiz in the 6th

b-Singled to left for B. Donnelly in the 8th

HR-R. Aurilia, B. Bonds

c-Flied out to left for J. Witasick in the 4th; d-Flied out to left for A. Fultz in the 6th; e-Struck out swinging for S. Eyre in the 9th

Anaheim	004	401	010	—10
San Francisco	100	030	000	—4

Anaheim	IP	H	R	ER	BB	SO	HR	ERA
R. Ortiz W	5	5	4	4	4	3	2	7.2
B. Donnelly	2	0	0	0	2	0	0	0
S. Schoeneweis	2	1	0	0	0	2	0	0

San Francisco	IP	H	R	ER	BB	SO	HR	ERA
L. Hernandez L	3 2/3	5	6	5	5	3	0	12.27
J. Witasick	1/3	3	2	2	1	1	0	54.01
A. Fultz	2	3	1	1	1	0	0	3.86
F. Rodriguez	1	1	0	0	0	0	0	4.5
S. Eyre	2	4	1	0	1	1	0	0

Rather, the Angels proved little ball works just fine, too—especially at the major league park where the fewest homers were hit this year.

"We scored a lot of runs today and we didn't hit any home runs. We have a lot of guys that are gap hitters," Spiezio said.

Every Angels starter except winning pitcher Ramon Ortiz got a hit. No DH, no worry. And they coasted despite setting a nine-inning Series record by leaving 15 runners on base.

"We want everyone to be a part of it," Angels slugger Troy Glaus said. "We're not trying to hit home runs; we just want to keep the line moving."

Hernandez was chased after 3 2/3 innings, the worst start of a glittery postseason career that had seen him go 6-0. Instead, he looked like the pitcher who tied for the NL lead in losses, which he did with 16.

The Angels scored four times in the third and four more in the fourth for an 8-1 lead. Spiezio, who dyed Angel red streaks into his hair and goatee before Game 1, was in the middle of both big innings.

After an error by sure-handed third baseman David Bell paved the way in the third, Spiezio lined a two-run triple to the deepest part of the field. The ball rolled to the 421-foot mark at the oddly angled corner in right center field.

Hernandez was pulled after Garret Anderson's RBI grounder in the fourth, set up when the Angels alertly pulled a double steal after the Giants' infield overshifted to the right side.

The Angels poured it on with hits against—and off—reliever Jay Witasick. Spiezio pulled a ball to right, Adam Kennedy hit a liner off Witasick's right elbow and Bengie Molina delivered Anaheim's third straight RBI single.

David Eckstein hit an RBI single in the sixth and the Angels added a run in the eighth when the Giants botched a comebacker.

Benito Santiago gave San Francisco a 1-0 lead in the first with a slow groundout. The Angels intentionally walked Bonds with one out and runners at first and third to bring up Santiago.

"We didn't really want Barry to have a chance early to break it open," Scioscia said.

"EVERYBODY KNOWS THAT ONE RUN ISN'T ENOUGH, TWO RUNS AREN'T ENOUGH. NO MATTER HOW MANY RUNS
WE SCORE, WE'RE GOING TO GO UP THERE AND ACT LIKE THAT'S THE BIGGEST AT-BAT WE'VE EVER HAD."

—SCOTT SPIEZIO

BELL HELPS GIANTS EVEN WORLD SERIES

BY BEN WALKER, AP SPORTS WRITER

The San Francisco Giants proved the Kid was really Mr. Hittable, after all.

And just in time.

David Bell lined a tie-breaking single off rookie sensation Francisco Rodriguez in the eighth inning and the Giants rallied past the Anaheim Angels 4-3, tying the World Series at two games each.

Down early and in danger of being blown out again, the Giants somehow slowed down Anaheim's persistent hitters.

And then, the biggest surprise of all: The Giants broke through against Rodriguez, who had been known as Mr. Unhittable, and Bell became the latest son to honor his major league father with a big hit in this Series.

"I was just trying to get a pitch I could handle and hit it hard," Bell said. "I don't know, he's had a lot of success so far. He's done a great job for these guys."

"So to get a win tonight was big," he said. "I think to get a run off him is important, too."

Officially, it was an unearned run because of a passed ball on Bengie Molina. No matter, it counted all the same as Giants came back from a 3-0 deficit and

posted their first Series win at home since 1962, setting off foghorn blasts from the nearby bay.

"You're not going to win every time," Rodriguez said. "I felt great, I made a couple of mistakes. They took advantage. Today, my stuff was good.

"You're going to have your bad days, your lucky days," he said. "I'll forget it, it's in the past, come back strong tomorrow."

"You're just trying to get to a young pitcher, maybe knock him off his pedestal," San Francisco's Jeff Kent said. "He's had a clean playoff slate, and we were hoping to dirty it a little bit."

Rodriguez set down Barry Bonds while pitching a perfect seventh, but the 20-year-old with a wicked slider and crackling fastball soon absorbed his first major league loss.

Rodriguez had blown away all 12 San Francisco hitters he faced until J.T. Snow singled to start the eighth. Snow moved up when Molina let a fastball skip off his mitt, but stayed put when first baseman Scott Spiezio made a sensational, diving catch on Reggie Sanders' foul bunt.

FINAL
ANAHEIM ANGELS 3, AT SAN FRANCISCO GIANTS 4

ANAHEIM	AB	R	H	RBI	SAN FRANCISCO	AB	R	H	RBI
D. Eckstein SS	3	0	0	1	K. Lofton CF	4	1	3	0
D. Erstad CF	4	0	0	0	R. Aurilia SS	4	1	3	1
T. Salmon RF	4	0	1	0	J. Kent 2B	3	0	0	1
G. Anderson LF	4	1	2	0	B. Bonds LF	1	0	0	0
T. Glaus 3B	4	1	1	2	B. Santiago C	4	0	1	1
S. Spiezio 1B	4	0	1	0	J. Snow 1B	4	1	1	0
B. Gil 2B	3	1	2	0	R. Sanders RF	4	0	1	0
b-A. Kennedy PH	1	0	1	0	D. Bell 3B	4	0	2	1
B. Molina C	3	0	1	0	K. Rueter P	2	1	1	0
c-B. Fullmer PH	1	0	0	0	d-T. Goodwin PH	0	0	0	0
J. Lackey P	2	0	1	0	F. Rodriguez P	0	0	0	0
B. Weber P	0	0	0	0	T. Worrell P	0	0	0	0
a-O. Palmeiro PH	1	0	0	0	e-R. Martinez PH	1	0	0	0
F. Rodriguez P	0	0	0	0	R. Nen P	0	0	0	0
Totals	34	3	10	3	Totals	31	4	12	4

HR-T. Glaus

a-Struck out swinging for B. Weber in the 7th; b-Singled to right for B. Gil in the 9th; c-Grounded to shortstop for B. Molina in the 9th

d-Walked for K. Rueter in the 6th
e-Struck out swinging for T. Worrell in the 8th

Anaheim	012	000	000	—3	
San Francisco	000	030	01x	—4	

Anaheim	IP	H	R	ER	BB	SO	HR	ERA
J. Lackey	5	9	3	3	3	2	0	6.14
B. Weber	1	1	0	0	1	0	0	5.4
F. Rodriguez L	2	2	1	0	0	2	0	0

San Francisco	IP	H	R	ER	BB	SO	HR	ERA
K. Rueter	6	9	3	3	0	2	1	4.5
F. Rodriguez	1	0	0	0	0	1	0	3.6
T. Worrell W	1	1	0	0	0	0	0	0
R. Nen S	1	1	0	0	0	0	0	0

Bell singled sharply past diving shortstop David Eckstein and Snow scored ahead of center fielder Darin Erstad's throw, setting off a celebration at Pacific Bell Park.

"I don't think you can look at what Francisco didn't do. Those guys are good hitters," Angels manager Mike Scioscia said.

Tim Worrell got the win and Robb Nen closed for a save.

Pitching on his 24th birthday, Angels rookie John Lackey picked up a nice present, the souvenir ball from his first major league hit. More importantly for Anaheim, he avoided trouble on the mound, thanks mostly to Benito Santiago.

Twice, Lackey intentionally walked Bonds to load the bases with one out. Both times, he got Santiago to hit grounders to Eckstein that the shortstop turned into inning-ending double plays.

"When I hit into the second double play, I didn't even want to go back to the dugout," Santiago said. "I felt like jumping into the stands and sitting with the fans."

Yet Santiago got sweet redemption with an RBI single that capped a three-run fifth that made it 3-all. And in a tasty twist for a Series dominated by long balls, the comeback started with two of the shortest hits yet.

Pitcher Kirk Rueter led off with a high chopper that he beat out for an infield single. Kenny Lofton followed with a bunt that slowly danced down the chalk line until third baseman Troy Glaus picked it up for another little single.

Rich Aurilia singled home the Giants' first run, Kent hit a sacrifice fly, and after another intentional walk to Bonds, Santiago singled up the middle. The MVP of the NL championship series clapped his hands and pointed toward the San Francisco dugout after rounding first base.

"Benito's come through big time in the second half," Giants manager Dusty Baker said.

Glaus hit a two-run shot, tying Bonds' record of seven home runs in a postseason, to give the

Angels a 3-0 lead in the third.

With runners on first and second and one out in the second, Lackey fouled off a bunt attempt. Undaunted with two strikes, he expertly took a low-and-away fastball the other way to right for a single that loaded the bases. Eckstein's sacrifice fly made it 1-0.

A leadoff single by Tim Salmon set up Glaus' third homer of the Series, a shot to center over the leaping Lofton.

GIANTS TAKE 3-2 LEAD OVER ANGELS

BY BEN WALKER, AP SPORTS WRITER

Teased and taunted for tiptoeing around Barry Bonds, the Anaheim Angels decided to challenge him.

Whack!

Bonds lined an RBI double that sent the San Francisco Giants zooming to a big lead that not even these pesky Angels could overcome, winning 16-4 in Game 5 to take a 3-2 lead in the World Series.

Jeff Kent sealed it with a pair of two-run homers, starting the party in full force at Pac Bell Park and putting the Giants on the brink of their first World Series title since Willie Mays & Co. won it for New York in 1954.

Rich Aurilia's three-run homer in the eighth gave the Giants the most runs by a team in a Series game since the New York Yankees walloped Pittsburgh 16-3 in 1960. It was the 17th homer overall by the Angels and San Francisco, tying a Series record, and set off a fog horn blast and shots from water cannons on top of the right field wall.

Once again, it took only one big swing by Bonds—Mays' godson—to swing the momentum in this Series. But, really, the Angels were caught in a lose-lose squeeze from the start.

They pitched to Bonds in the first inning, and the Giants got three runs. They intentionally walked him in the second, and San Francisco scored three more.

Halloween was still a week away, but the big guy in orange and black had plenty of tricks and few treats for Anaheim.

A sellout crowd of 42,713, tense when the Angels climbed back from a 6-0 deficit and brought the tying run to the plate in the middle innings, erupted when Kent connected in the sixth and again in the seventh.

"We never give in. We started ahead right away, but these guys never give up either," said Benito Santiago, who drove in three runs for the Giants.

Bonds added another double and a single and Kenny Lofton sprinkled in a two-run triple as the Giants pulled away.

Chad Zerbe got the win, relieving when Jason Schmidt was pulled in the fifth, one out short of qualifying for his second win of the Series. Schmidt struck out eight, yet Giants manager Dusty Baker took no chances after Troy Glaus' RBI double made it 6-3.

Jarrod Washburn, who lost to Schmidt in the opener, absorbed another defeat.

FINAL
ANAHEIM ANGELS 4, AT SAN FRANCISCO GIANTS 16

ANAHEIM	AB	R	H	RBI	SAN FRANCISCO	AB	R	H	RBI
D. Eckstein SS	4	1	2	1	K. Lofton CF	6	3	3	2
D. Erstad CF	4	0	1	1	S. Eyre P	0	0	0	0
T. Salmon RF	4	1	1	0	R. Aurilia SS	6	2	2	3
A. Ochoa RF	1	0	0	0	J. Kent 2B	5	4	3	4
G. Anderson LF	5	0	1	0	B. Bonds LF	4	2	3	1
T. Glaus 3B	4	0	1	1	B. Santiago C	3	0	1	3
S. Spiezio 1B	2	0	0	0	R. Sanders RF	1	0	0	1
S. Shields P	0	0	0	0	F. Rodriguez P	0	0	0	0
A. Kennedy 2B	4	0	0	0	c-S. Dunston PH	1	0	0	0
B. Molina C	4	1	1	0	T. Worrell P	0	0	0	0
J. Molina C	0	0	0	0	d-P. Feliz PH	1	0	0	0
J. Washburn P	1	0	0	0	T. Goodwin RF	0	0	0	0
a-O. Palmeiro PH	1	1	1	0	J. Snow 1B	4	2	2	0
B. Donnelly P	0	0	0	0	D. Bell 3B	3	2	2	1
b-B. Gil PH	1	0	1	0	J. Schmidt P	1	0	0	0
B. Weber P	0	0	0	0	C. Zerbe P	0	0	0	0
S. Wooten 1B	1	0	1	0	T. Shinjo RF-CF	2	1	0	0
Totals	36	4	10	3	Totals	37	16	16	15

a-Doubled to right for J. Washburn in the 5th; b-Doubled to deep center for B. Donnelly in the 6th

c-Struck out swinging for F. Rodriguez in the 6th
d-Flied out to right for T. Worrell in the 8th

HR-J. Kent 2, R. Aurilia

Anaheim	000	031	000 —4
San Francisco	330	002	44x —16

Anaheim	IP	H	R	ER	BB	SO	HR	ERA
J. Washburn L	4	6	6	6	5	1	0	9.31
B. Donnelly	1	0	0	0	0	2	0	0
B. Weber	1 1/3	5	5	5	1	2	1	13.5
S. Shields	1 2/3	5	5	1	0	1	2	5.4

San Francisco	IP	H	R	ER	BB	SO	HR	ERA
J. Schmidt	4 2/3	7	3	3	3	8	0	5.23
C. Zerbe W	1	2	1	1	0	0	0	3.6
F. Rodriguez	1/3	0	0	0	0	0	0	3.37
T. Worrell	2	1	0	0	0	2	0	0
S. Eyre	1	0	0	0	0	1	0	0

Friendly, respectful rivals for four games, the teams turned edgy for Game 5.

After giving up two homers to Glaus in the opener, Schmidt spun him to the dirt with a 97 mph fastball in the first inning. Glaus got up, struck out with runners at the corners for the third out and flung his bat toward the dugout.

Lofton led off with a single and Washburn made his first critical mistake, walking Kent on a full count with one out.

Up stepped Bonds and just like in Game 1, when he gave up a home run to the slugger, Washburn decided to pitch to him.

The count went to 2-1 and Washburn backed off the mound, taking a moment to compose himself as the crowd chanted, "Barry! Barry!" When Washburn left his next pitch out over the plate, Bonds lined an RBI double that rolled to the wall in right field, and the rout was on.

Santiago followed with a sacrifice fly and Anaheim manager Mike Scioscia played the percentages,

intentionally walking Reggie Sanders. But Washburn couldn't take advantage of the lefty vs. lefty matchup and walked J.T. Snow to load the bases, prompting a visit from pitching coach Bud Black.

That didn't help, as Washburn also walked Game 4 star David Bell to force home another run that made it 3-0.

San Francisco kept pouring it on in the second after another leadoff single by Lofton. Center fielder Darin Erstad made his second outstanding catch to rob Aurilia, yet that only delayed what was coming.

Kent doubled off the right field wall and the Angels took no chances with Bonds this time, throwing four wide ones while Giants fans razzed Washburn by waving rubber chickens.

Santiago spoiled the strategy with a two-run single.

Only then did the Angels start warming up someone in the bullpen, and as Scot Shields got loose, Sanders hit a sacrifice fly for a 6-0 lead.

SPIEZIO SPARKS ANGELS' VICTORY

BY JOHN NADEL, AP SPORTS WRITER

The Anaheim Angels didn't start hitting until the seventh inning in Game 6 of the World Series.

Once Scott Spiezio got the Angels going, they were unstoppable.

Spiezio hit a three-run homer off Felix Rodriguez in the seventh, and the Angels scored three more times in the eighth to beat the San Francisco Giants 6-5 and force a decisive Game 7.

The Angels' rally from five runs down was the biggest in Series history for a team facing elimination.

"I didn't hit it perfect, I hit it enough to get it over," said Spiezio, who has 19 RBIs to tie the postseason record set by Cleveland's Sandy Alomar Jr. five years ago.

"I was praying, I was saying, 'God, please, just get it over the fence.' Seemed like it took forever," Spiezio said. "Rodriguez has been tough on me this whole series. He's been in every game. Seems like I faced him every time he's come in. I haven't hit one on the barrel yet, I've just missed some balls."

He didn't miss this one.

Spiezio, 1 for 15 for a .733 average with runners in scoring position in the postseason, worked the count full before hitting his homer on Rodriguez's eighth pitch—a low fastball.

"It was a good pitch, but the guy's a good hitter, you know?" Rodriguez said.

Spiezio is 4 for 5 with runners in scoring position in the World Series.

Manager Mike Scioscia and hitting coach Mickey Hatcher have often spoke of the Angels' resilience.

Never was it more apparent than Saturday night.

FINAL

SAN FRANCISCO GIANTS 5, AT ANAHEIM ANGELS 6

SAN FRANCISCO	AB	R	H	RBI	ANAHEIM	AB	R	H	RBI
K. Lofton CF	5	2	2	0	D. Eckstein SS	4	0	0	0
R. Aurilia SS	4	0	0	0	D. Erstad CF	3	1	1	1
J. Kent 2B	4	0	2	1	T. Salmon RF	4	0	2	0
B. Bonds LF	2	1	1	1	C. Figgins PR	0	1	0	0
B. Santiago C	3	0	0	0	A. Ochoa RF	0	0	0	0
J. Snow 1B	4	0	1	0	G. Anderson LF	4	1	1	0
R. Sanders RF	4	0	0	0	T. Glaus 3B	3	1	2	2
D. Bell 3B	4	1	1	0	B. Fullmer DH	4	1	1	0
S. Dunston DH	3	1	1	2	S. Spiezio 1B	3	1	1	3
a-T. Goodwin PH	1	0	0	0	B. Molina C	2	0	0	0
Totals	34	5	8	4	a-O. Palmeiro PH	1	0	0	0
					J. Molina C	0	0	0	0
					A. Kennedy 2B	4	0	2	0
					Totals	32	6	10	6

HR-S. Dunston, B. Bonds

a-Struck out swinging for S. Dunston in the 9th

HR-S. Spiezio, D. Erstad

a-Struck out swinging for B. Molina in the 7th

San Francisco	000	031	100	—5		
Anaheim	000	000	33x	—6		

San Francisco	IP	H	R	ER	BB	SO	HR	ERA
R. Ortiz	6 1/3	4	2	2	2	2	0	10.12
F. Rodriguez	1/3	1	1	1	0	1	1	4.76
S. Eyre	0	1	0	0	0	0	0	0
T. Worrell L	1/3	3	3	2	0	0	1	3.86
R. Nen	1	1	0	0	1	2	0	0

Anaheim	IP	H	R	ER	BB	SO	HR	ERA
K. Appier	4 1/3	4	3	3	3	2	1	11.37
F. Rodriguez	2 2/3	4	2	2	0	4	1	2.35
B. Donnelly W	1	0	0	0	1	2	0	0
T. Percival S	1	0	0	0	0	2	0	4.5

S. Eyre pitched to 1 batter in the 7th. T. Worrell pitched to 3 batters in the 8th.

"I could sit back as a coach and try to come up with philosophies," Hatcher said. "I am speechless, I just don't know what to say. I'm in awe. 'Get somebody on, get something going.' That's their motto."

The Giants seemed a lock to win their first Series since 1954 when Russ Ortiz, armed with a 5-0 lead, struck out Garret Anderson to begin the seventh.

Ortiz had allowed only two hits and faced three over the minimum at that point.

That's when the Angels came alive.

First it was Troy Glaus and Brad Fullmer with singles, putting an end to Ortiz's night.

Then, the switch-hitting Spiezio hit a high fly into the right-field seats—just beyond the reach of Reggie Sanders—to cut the Giants' lead to two runs.

"I was in the on-deck circle, I didn't think it was going," Anaheim's Bengie Molina said. "It just kept carrying, carrying, carrying."

Darin Erstad homered off Tim Worrell to open the eighth, giving the Angels 24 homers in their 16 postseason games.

Tim Salmon and Garret Anderson followed with singles, with left fielder Barry Bonds' error allowing Anderson to reach second after pinch runner Chone Figgins went to third.

Giants manager Dusty Baker opted for closer Robb Nen, and Glaus foiled the strategy by hitting a two-run double to left center to put the Angels ahead.

Troy Percival blanked San Francisco in the ninth for his sixth postseason save in as many chances.

"You're battling out to out. Our bullpen has been taxed a little bit. We're getting it done," Scioscia said. "I thought if we could get some hits strung together, we could get back in the game. I didn't know it would happen as quickly as it did. It was great to see."

World Series, Game 7
Angels 4, Giants 1 at Edison Field

ANGELS IN SEVENTH HEAVEN!

BY BEN WALKER, AP SPORTS WRITER

Darin Erstad caught the fly ball for the final out of Game 7, and the mayhem began.

The Anaheim Angels whooped it up like Little Leaguers, celebrating their first World Series championship with hugs, slaps and unabashed joy.

Watching it all from a dark corner of the Giants' dugout was the best hitter in the world. Barry Bonds knew this moment could have been his.

"You want the results to be different," the San Francisco star said. "They outplayed us, they deserve it. They beat us. They're world champions."

Improbable ones, at that.

Behind rookie starter John Lackey and a big hit by Garret Anderson, the Angels pulled it off, beating the Giants 4-1 to finally win the crown after 42 years.

"These fans have been waiting a long, long time for this," MVP Troy Glaus said. "And I know we're all happy to be part of the team to bring it to them."

The highest scoring Series in history came down to pitching, as it always seems to do in October. And Lackey and the bullpen gave Anaheim enough to win baseball's first all-wild card matchup.

The Angels became the eighth straight home team to win Game 7 of the World Series. History was on their side from the start and so was an omen—a skywriting plane put a gigantic halo over Edison Field before the first pitch.

The Rally Monkey was ready, but the mascot only showed up a couple of times on the video scoreboard.

"We love the monkey because of what it does for us. It's a good-luck charm," Lackey said. "But it's good not to see him because that means we're winning."

Lackey, pitching on three days' rest, became only the second rookie starter to win Game 7 of the Series. He joined Babe Adams, who pitched Pittsburgh past Ty Cobb and Detroit in 1909.

Anderson, now due to get the recognition he's always deserved, hit a three-run double off Livan Hernandez in the third for a 4-1 lead.

"Well, I just wanted to get into a situation where I'd be able to hit my pitch, not do too much," Anderson said.

FINAL

SAN FRANCISCO GIANTS 1, AT ANAHEIM ANGELS 4

SAN FRANCISCO	AB	R	H	RBI	ANAHEIM	AB	R	H	RBI
K. Lofton CF	4	0	0	0	D. Eckstein SS	3	1	1	0
R. Aurilia SS	4	0	0	0	D. Erstad CF	3	1	1	0
J. Kent 2B	4	0	0	0	T. Salmon RF	2	1	0	0
B. Bonds LF	3	0	1	0	A. Ochoa RF	0	0	0	0
B. Santiago C	3	1	2	0	G. Anderson LF	4	0	1	3
J. Snow 1B	4	0	3	0	T. Glaus 3B	2	0	0	0
R. Sanders RF	1	0	0	1	B. Fullmer DH	4	0	0	0
a-T. Goodwin PH-RF	2	0	0	0	S. Spiezio 1B	3	1	0	0
D. Bell 3B	3	0	0	0	B. Molina C	3	0	2	1
P. Feliz DH	3	0	0	0	A. Kennedy 2B	3	0	0	0
b-T. Shinjo PH	1	0	0	0	Totals	27	4	5	4
Totals	32	1	6	1					

a-Struck out swinging for R. Sanders in the 6th; b-Struck out swinging for P. Feliz in the the 9th

San Francisco	010	000	000	—1
Anaheim	013	000	00x	—4

San Francisco	IP	H	R	ER	BB	SO	HR	ERA
L. Hernandez L	2	4	4	4	4	1	0	14.29
C. Zerbe	1	0	0	0	0	0	0	3
K. Rueter	4	1	0	0	1	3	0	2.7
T. Worrell	1	0	0	0	0	1	0	3.18

Anaheim	IP	H	R	ER	BB	SO	HR	ERA
J. Lackey W	5	4	1	1	1	4	0	4.38
B. Donnelly	2	1	0	0	1	2	0	0
F. Rodriguez	1	0	0	0	1	3	0	2.08
T. Percival S	1	1	0	0	1	1	0	3

L. Hernandez pitched to 5 batters in the 3rd

Brendan Donnelly, Francisco Rodriguez and Troy Percival closed it for manager Mike Scioscia's bunch. Percival escaped a two-on, one-out jam for his third save of the Series.

"Unbelievable for us, for our fans," Percival said. "This team has worked as hard as any team ever. We deserve it."

It was particularly sweet for Scioscia, who won a title with Baker as players in 1981 for the Los Angeles Dodgers, the team that long overshadowed the neighbors to the south.

"I'm enjoying it, but what these guys have done—they're going to enjoy it for a long time," Scioscia said.

After the game, Scioscia and Baker spoke on the phone.

"We had everything fall into place," Scioscia said. "If we didn't win it, you know I wanted you to. You guys are champions, hold your heads high. You're awesome."

Beloved owner Gene Autry never saw his team get this far before passing away, and it didn't look like these guys would do it, either, especially after finishing 41 games out of first place in 2001.

Somehow, the Angels pulled it together. They led the majors in hitting, overwhelmed the New York Yankees and Minnesota in the AL playoffs and then knocked out Bonds and Co.

"Somewhere, Gene Autry is smiling right now," commissioner Bud Selig said as he presented the trophy.

Anaheim and the Giants combined for a record 85 runs and 21 homers. Hernandez had been

6-0 lifetime in the postseason before losing twice to the Angels.

Hernandez walked Scott Spiezio with two outs in the second and Bengie Molina followed with a double that tied it at 1.

Molina added another double, and the hits were his way of honoring his father, who was far away. Earlier Sunday, former amateur outfielder Benjamin Molina Santana was in Puerto Rico, where he was inducted into the island's hall of fame.

TROY GLAUS·WORLD SERIES MVP

BY RONALD BLUM, AP SPORTS WRITER

Troy Glaus felt young again, a World Series MVP as happy as a little boy.

"This is why we put all the time and effort in," he said, recalling a time long ago. "All the swings against the garage door when you were a kid."

Those swings he had spent two decades perfecting helped Anaheim win the World Series and Glaus win the MVP award. He beat Barry Bonds 4-1 in the vote after batting .385 with three doubles, three home runs and eight RBIs.

"At this point, I don't even really know how I'm feeling except ecstatic," Glaus said.

He is the Angels' fire, the one who throws tantrums in defeat. He flings his helmet, his bat.

He's not going to toss the World Series MVP trophy.

When he was told he won the award, it really didn't sink in.

"I was just so excited about being world champion," he said after Anaheim's 4-1 victory over San Francisco. "I didn't even really know what to think."

And when the championship was securely in the Angels' hands, what made him happiest was coming through for those halo-wearing, monkey-waving fans, some coming to games for four decades, hoping for this moment.

"These fans have been waiting a long, long time for this," Glaus said. "And I know we're all happy to be part of the team to bring it to them."

"Actually, we've had that way of thinking all year," Glaus said. "No matter what we came up against, we were going to play hard and leave it all out there, and that's what we did here."

On a team where many players stood out, Glaus had the most consistent Series, going 10 for 26 at the plate.

He homered twice in Anaheim's opening 4-3 loss and hit a two-run drive in Game 4, another 4-3 defeat.

His biggest hit didn't go over the wall, but instead swung the momentum of the Series.

When he came up in the eighth inning of Game 6 Saturday night, with the Angels having clawed back to 5-4 after trailing by five runs, his two-run double off Robb Nen sent the Angels on to a 6-5 win and gave them life when they could have been going home.

"I think the feeling would be tremendous no matter where we were," he said, "but for me to be at home, my friends and family get to be here. They've all been a part of it. For them to be watching, and the fan support and everything—unbelievable."

AT BAT 1   AVG. .296   BANK OF THE WEST   8:19   TOYO

2002 REGULAR SEASON STATISTICS
BATTING

Name	GP	AB	R	H	2B	3B	HR	RBI	SB	AVG
Alfredo Amezaga	12	13	3	7	2	0	0	2	1	.538
Adam Kennedy	144	474	65	148	32	6	7	52	17	.312
Garrett Anderson	158	638	93	195	56	3	29	123	6	.306
Orlando Palmeiro	110	263	35	79	12	1	0	31	7	.300
David Eckstein	152	608	107	178	22	6	8	63	21	.293
Shawn Wooten	49	113	13	33	8	0	3	19	2	.292
Brad Fullmer	130	429	75	124	35	6	19	59	10	.289
Jose Nieves	45	97	17	28	2	0	0	6	1	.289
Tim Salmon	138	483	84	138	37	1	22	88	6	.286
Scott Spiezio	153	491	80	140	34	2	12	82	6	.285
Benji Gil	61	130	11	37	8	1	3	20	2	.285
Darin Erstad	150	625	99	177	28	4	10	73	23	.283
Julio Ramirez	29	32	6	9	0	1	1	7	0	.281
Alex Ochoa	37	65	8	18	7	0	2	10	2	.277
Jose Molina	29	70	5	19	3	0	0	5	0	.271
Troy Glaus	156	569	99	142	24	1	30	111	10	.250
Bengi Molina	122	428	34	105	18	0	5	47	0	.245
Jorge Fabregas	35	88	8	17	1	0	0	8	0	.193
Jeff DaVanon	16	30	3	5	3	0	1	4	1	.167
Chone Figgins	15	12	6	2	1	0	0	1	2	.167
Clay Bellinger	2	1	0	0	0	0	0	0	0	.000
Totals	162	5658	851	1601	333	32	152	811	117	.282

PITCHING

Name	W	L	G	SV	CG	IP	H	BB	K	ERA
Francisco Rodriguez	0	0	5	0	0	5.2	3	2	13	0.00
Troy Percival	4	1	58	40	0	56.1	38	25	68	1.92
Brendan Donnelly	1	1	46	1	0	49.2	32	19	54	2.17
Scot Shields	5	3	29	0	0	49.0	31	21	30	2.20
Ben Weber	7	2	63	7	0	78.0	70	22	43	2.54
Jarrod Washburn	18	6	32	0	1	206.0	183	59	139	3.15
Lou Pote	0	2	31	0	0	50.1	33	26	32	3.22
Matt Wise	0	0	7	0	0	8.1	7	1	6	3.24
Dennis Cook	1	1	37	0	0	24.0	21	10	13	3.38
John Lackey	9	4	18	0	1	108.1	113	33	69	3.66
Ramon Ortiz	15	9	32	0	4	217.1	188	68	162	3.77
Mark Lukasiewicz	2	0	17	0	0	14.0	17	9	15	3.86
Kevin Appier	14	12	32	0	0	188.1	191	64	132	3.92
Mickey Callaway	2	1	6	0	0	34.1	31	11	23	4.19
Al Levine	4	4	52	5	0	63.2	61	34	40	4.24
Scott Schoeneweis	9	8	54	1	0	118.0	119	49	65	4.88
Aaron Sele	8	9	26	0	1	160.0	190	49	82	4.89
Donne Wall	0	0	17	0	0	21.0	17	7	13	6.43
Totals	99	63	162	54	7	1449.3	1345	509	999	3.69

2002 POSTSEASON STATISTICS
BATTING

Name	GP	AB	R	H	2B	3B	HR	RBI	SB	AVG
Chone Figgins	6	1	4	1	0	0	0	0	1	1.000
Benji Gil	6	12	2	8	1	0	0	1	0	.667
John Lackey	1	2	0	1	0	0	0	0	0	.500
Shawn Wooten	9	19	5	9	0	0	1	3	0	.474
Darin Erstad	16	71	14	25	5	0	2	7	3	.352
Troy Glaus	16	61	15	21	3	1	7	13	0	.344
Adam Kennedy	15	47	10	16	3	0	4	10	1	.340
Scott Spiezio	16	55	10	18	4	1	3	19	1	.327
G. Anderson	16	70	11	21	4	0	2	13	0	.300
Brad Fullmer	12	34	6	10	3	0	1	5	2	.294
D. Eckstein	16	68	9	20	0	0	0	6	2	.294
Tim Salmon	16	59	10	17	2	0	4	12	1	.288
Bengie Molina	16	50	2	13	4	1	0	6	0	.260
O. Palmeiro	6	6	1	1	1	0	0	0	0	.167
Alex Ochoa	12	5	2	0	0	0	0	0	0	.000
J. Washburn	1	1	0	0	0	0	0	0	0	.000
S. Schoeneweis	1	0	0	0	0	0	0	0	0	.000
Ramon Ortiz	1	3	0	0	0	0	0	0	0	.000
Jose Molina	6	1	0	0	0	0	0	0	0	.000
Ben Weber	2	0	0	0	0	0	0	0	0	.000
Scot Shields	1	0	0	0	0	0	0	0	0	.000
B. Donnelly	2	0	0	0	0	0	0	0	0	.000
F. Rodriguez	1	0	0	0	0	0	0	0	0	.000
Angels	16	565	101	181	30	3	24	95	11	.320

PITCHING

Name	W	L	G	SV	IP	H	BB	K	ERA
F. Rodriguez	5	1	11	0	18.2	10	5	28	1.93
John Lackey	2	0	5	0	22.1	21	6	17	2.42
Troy Percival	0	0	9	7	9.2	8	1	10	2.79
S. Schoeneweis	0	0	6	0	3.0	3	1	2	3.00
B. Donnelly	1	0	11	0	13.0	7	5	13	4.15
J. Washburn	1	2	5	0	28.2	30	10	17	5.02
Scot Shields	0	0	1	0	1.2	5	0	1	5.40
Kevin Appier	0	1	5	0	21.2	24	12	10	6.23
Ramon Ortiz	2	0	3	0	13.0	18	9	7	9.00
Ben Weber	0	1	9	0	8.1	15	4	8	10.80
Totals	11	5	16	7	140	141	53	113	4.82

PHOTO CREDITS
AP/WIDE WORLD PHOTOS